CATS
IN
BOOKS

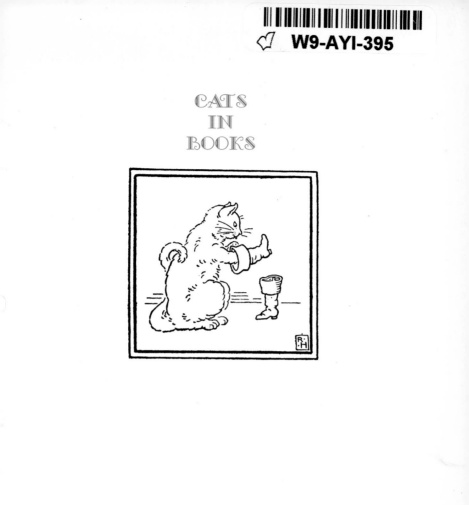

Dad's very fond of books,
    And as the Library is near,
He often goes to bring one home,—
A big one he has here.

Louis Wain.

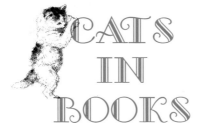

CATS IN BOOKS

*a celebration of cat illustration
through the ages*

SELECTED AND INTRODUCED BY
RODNEY DALE

THE BRITISH LIBRARY

First published 1997

This paperback edition first published 2008 by
The British Library
96 Euston Road
London NW1 2DB

ISBN 978 0 7123 5023 5

Printed and bound in Italy

Half-title R. Heighway 1895
Below The Cat and The Mouse (1894) illustrated by
Alice B Woodward.

Opposite from *The White Cat* (1847) see page 58.

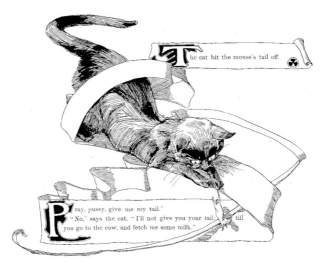

The cat bit the mouse's tail off.

"Pray, pussy, give me my tail."
"No," says the cat, "I'll not give you your tail, till
you go to the cow, and fetch me some milk."

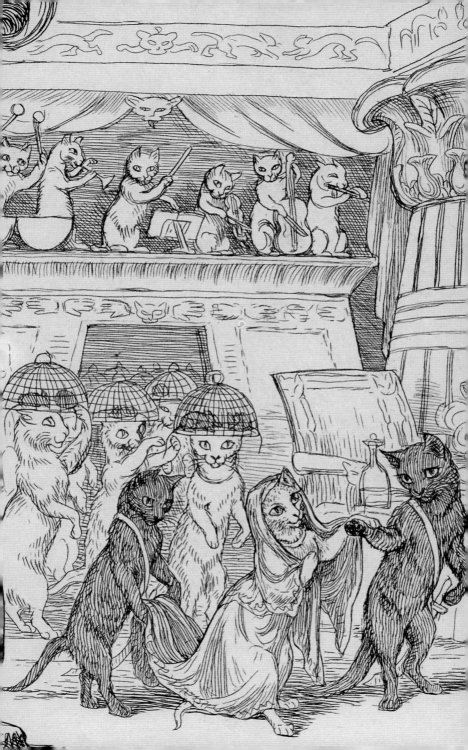

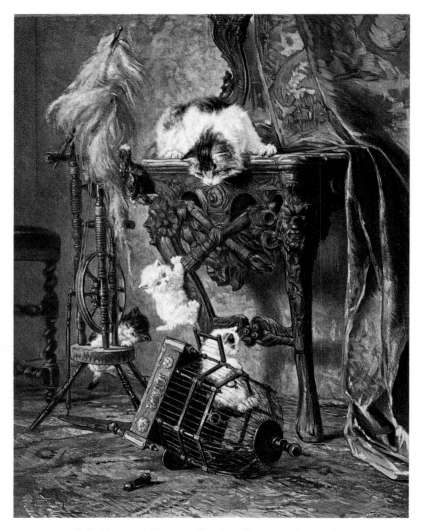

'Mischievious kittens' by Henriette Ronner – see page 84.
Madame Ronner's drawings embellish the Introduction.

Introduction   *Cats in Books* celebrates people's fascination with cats through the ages, particularly as it is reflected in manuscript and book illustration.

As is well known, cats were revered in Ancient Egypt, doubtless because of their work on rat-infested Egyptian grain stores. Murals of the period show cats kept as domestic pets but, because they were regarded as holy, they were sometimes sacrificed. However, their remains were reverently preserved afterwards, which presumably helped to assuage any feeling of guilt. Unfortunately, there are no Ancient Egyptian books from which we can reproduce illustrations.

It was forbidden to export cats from Egypt, so that any that were smuggled out acquired a special status in their new homes. Certainly they went on to live lives of lazy languor in other parts of the Mediterranean – in Greece and the Roman Empire – though little was written about them at that time. They do feature in the tales of Æsop [see pages 22 & 38] though this is not hard evidence because Æsop (like Nostradamus after him) has attracted new material through the centuries, perhaps to 'prove' how wise 'the ancients' were.

The domestic (Egyptian) cat (*Felis caffra*) spread from the Mediterranean – as did the rodents that were its prey; both cats and rodents were previously unknown in Europe. Maritime trading helped this spread; it was impossible to run a rat-free ship, and the ship's cat was an important member of the crew. The domestic cat *Felis domestica* – a species distinct from the fierce European wild cat *Felis catus* – was uncommon in Britain until the late Mediaeval period (about a millennium ago) when laws were passed to protect it because of its value in helping to preserve the hard-won harvest.

The cat was – and is – a creature of two worlds; in its first world it is an indoor creature, the playful kitten growing into the purring companion, taking over the best chair, entwining itself round your ankles (usually at feeding time), sharing your bed; in its second world it is an outdoor creature with sharp retractable claws, pointed teeth and super-efficient night vision, climbing trees, stalking, pouncing on anything that moves – and often re-crossing the boundary to the first world to lay out its catch for your approval. It is this very quality of leading a double life, part domestic and part secret, that makes cats both mysterious and endearing – and makes them such excellent subjects for writers and artists.

The Christian Church had a love–hate relationship with the cat. *Ancrene Riwle (The Rule of Nuns, 1230)* allows an anchoress (a female religious recluse) to keep a cat for companionship: 'Ye shall not possess any beast, my dear sisters, except only a cat'. Monasteries, too, were ideal places for cats – happy hunting grounds, and plenty of companionship. No wonder that we find cats, more or less stylised, in illuminated manuscripts. The earliest illus-

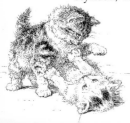

trations we reproduce are from fine manuscripts: the *Lindisfarne Gospels* [14] and the *Book of Kells* [16].

Notwithstanding their important secular roles as rat-catchers and companions, cats were still associated with paganism. It took the inhabitants of Britain a long time to forget the period of Roman rule, and the pagan gods the Romans had brought with them – for example, they had adopted the Egyptian cat-god Bast, and associated the cat on its nocturnal rounds with Diana, virgin huntress and moon-goddess; and later with Hecate, goddess of night, the moon, the underworld, childbirth and magic.

In time, cats came to be thought of as witches' 'familiars' – supernatural companions who manifested themselves as animals [28]. At first, the Church held that witchcraft was a delusion, but this benign view gradually turned to a fanatical fear of an anti-Christian conspiracy. From 1258, the Inquisition treated witchcraft as heresy, and in 1434 some 300 years of persecuting witches began. Persecution spread to America, with the celebrated case of the Witches of Salem in 1692. The last British execution for witchcraft was in 1684; the last in America in 1692.

A spreading belief in witchcraft is a phenomenon of self-delusion: witches are like old women who are like witches. In spite of a life of childbirth and child rearing, women have always tended to live longer than men, so old women are not uncommon. Hard work, and a lack of the benefits of modern dentistry and chiropody, are apt to produce old women of fearsome appearance and gait. If experience equals wisdom, old women are wise. And, living a solitary life, they may well seek, or accept, the friendship of cats.

Cats also had an ambivalent relationship with hearth and home. On the one hand, they might be buried alive in the foundations of a building to make it a happy (!) place; on the other (and more sensible) hand, they might be loved and cherished, thus bringing good luck. On the assumption that those who love and cherish cats are thoroughly nice people, harmony in the home would of course follow as the night the day.

Cats, reared from kittenhood by humans, apparently think of us as cats. As we talk to babies (preferably in adult terms), so do we talk to cats – and the cats talk back to us. Dogs are different; a terse vocabulary of Stay! Sit! and so on is good enough for them. Dogs don't have a secret life, and 'dog people' don't weave the same fantasies about their pets as 'cat people' do. When a cat goes out, it may be attending an orchestral performance – or even playing in the orchestra [39] – dancing [98], or taking part in other uplifting artistic activities.

There is thus little difficulty in seeing the cat as the 'power behind the throne' – as it appears in the story of Dick Whittington [30] (who helped his master to become Lord Mayor of London) and in Puss in Boots [50] (who translated his master from the third son of a poor miller

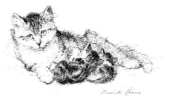

to a Prince of the Realm – and presumably, in due time, King). Essential to both these cats is the power to catch rodents, but whereas Whittington's cat does nothing other than that to help his master, Puss in Boots is an infinitely more roguish character; his prowess is a means to an end – first, to bring his master to the King's attention; later to secure him a fine castle.

For centuries, both farms and domestic buildings have had their working cats; the environment is as attractive to the rodents as to their predators. A good mouser was beyond price – and still is, if you have mice. The trappings of life have changed over the centuries, but human nature – the self within – has changed little. Similarly cats have, since time immemorial, been attracted to a warm corner, a supply of food, and sympathetic human company [88].

The Industrial Revolution of the eighteenth century resulted in the predominant environment changing from farming to trading, and people moving towards expanding towns. Concentrations of people lead to concentrations of foodstuffs and garbage – a fine environment for rodents, and hence again for cats. Edward Donovan [44] gives a vivid description of a nightly migration of rats from one old city property to another – crossing the rooftops, finding their way down inside the walls and behind the panelling – there was safety in numbers, and no cat dared to get in their way, but woe betide any stragglers. Fortunately, public hygiene improved through the nineteenth century, and cats became properly domesticated. The rodent population having been reduced considerably, all puss had to do was to eat, sleep, wash and be companionable. Interest in the cat *per se* grew; cats became better understood, and better fed and cared for and more rounded; other types of cats were imported and bred for strength and colour and pattern of coat; the cry of the cats'-meat man was heard in the land.

A cat show was held at St Giles's Fair, Winchester in 1598, but it was nearly 300 years before the next. On 13 July 1871 the writer, artist and great friend of the cat, Mr Harrison Weir [62] organised the first regular cat show at the Crystal Palace in London's Hyde Park. From then on, cat breeding and showing became all the rage, with the appropriate regulatory apparatus to register pedigrees and organise events, meetings, newsletters and the like. The first American cat show was held in New York's Madison Square Garden in 1895, and there are now cat societies and shows in most parts of the world.

It is difficult to determine in what ways the shape and appearance of the cat has changed over the centuries, and we might think that cat illustration could help us. Books on cats, and the cat tribe, are – hardly surprisingly – illustrated with pictures of their subjects, some believable, some questionable. We would expect, for example, Leonardo's cats [20] to be true to life, but there is no reason to suppose that Caxton's cats [22] are portraits of real animals. But did the Angora [42], drawn from a preserved skin, *really* look like Huet's picture of it?

The majority of cat illustrations in the last century or so are those accompanying stories for children or adults, and sometimes for both [66]. We cannot trust anything we see in this context as an accurate depiction of pussydom, though we may well learn something about the place of the cat in the society represented. There is no doubt that the appearance of the domestic cat has changed through the ages, but it is difficult to say how, and it may be more a function of good food, good breeding and a good home than of a steady evolution.

The last decade of the nineteenth century saw a boom in cats doing human things [78], an approach developed in their different ways by artist–writers such as Beatrix Potter [90], Kathleen Hale [96] and Graham Oakley [104]. The adventures of Beatrix Potter's Tom Kitten take place in a self-consistent rural animal world. Kathleen Hale's Orlando is proactive, and makes human-type things happen in a cat world. Graham Oakley's Sampson is dedicated to looking after his friends (the Church Mice) as they are all affected by the machinations of the human world. As the Twentieth Century draws to a close, the cat has a firmer place in human affection and culture than ever before. It is with enormous pleasure that we are able to present this survey of Cats in Books.

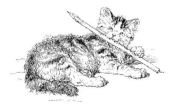

The Lindisfarne Gospels

This manuscript of the four Gospels in Latin was probably written in the year 698 to mark the canonisation of Cuthbert, abbot of Lindisfarne, who had died 20 years earlier. The *Gospels* were written by Eadfrith, bishop of Lindisfarne from 698 to 721, apparently a cat-lover with a sense of humour. The Cat is found on the initial page of Luke, its hind legs and tail at the top, its elongated body containing eight birds running down the right-hand margin, and its front legs and head at the bottom as shown. It is stalking a flock of birds on the other side of the page to add to its catch.

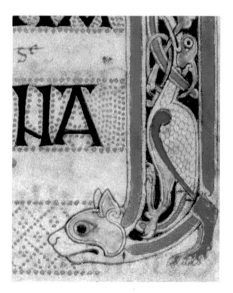

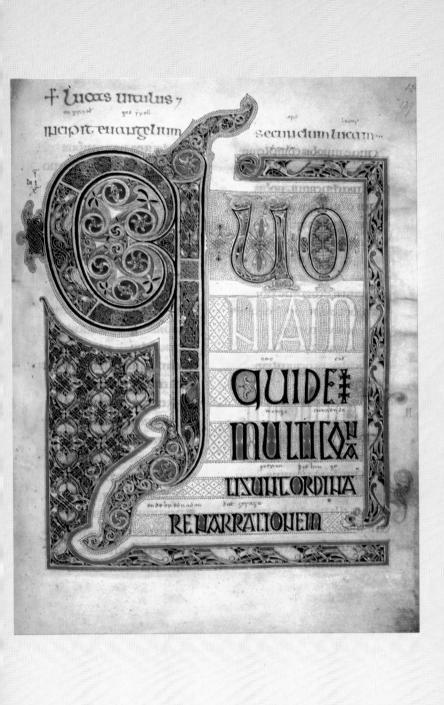

QUO
NIAM
QUIDE✠
MULTI
USUNT ORDINA
RENARRATIONEM

The Book of Kells

This manuscript of the four Gospels was written in the eighth or ninth century in a script known as Irish majuscule. It was probably written at the abbey of Kells, in the Irish county of Meath, which became the headquarters of the Columban community after the sack of the monastery at Iona by Vikings in 806. It has breathtaking illumination and illustration – intricate abstract patterns and animal forms – and there are several depictions of cats. A cornerpiece shows two cats clearly on good terms with a family of rats (or large mice); the multi-coloured cat (below) seems to be chasing a large rat which is running away with a wafer (used in Holy Communion) in its mouth.

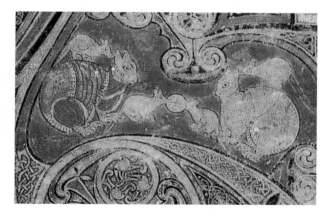

Right A finely-observed pair of wrestling cats which, though stylised, somehow contrive to look exactly like our own cats locked in friendly combat on the hearthrug 1,200 years later.

putatis quia ã

ut praeter om

tes inhierusal

si nonpoeniten

peric

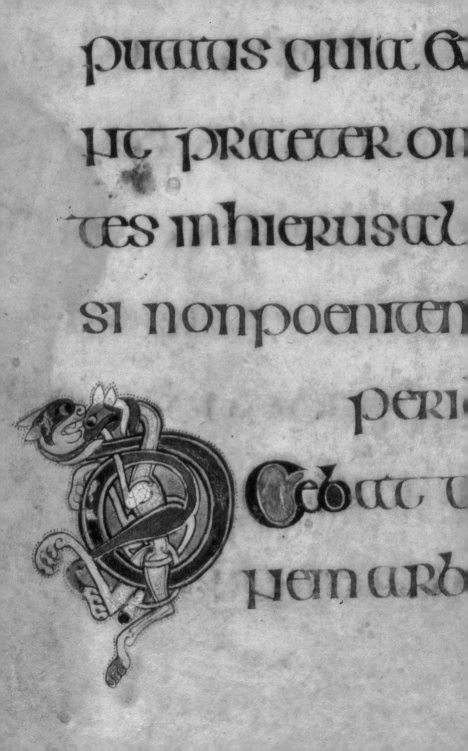Cebat u

pien urb

Psalter and Bestiary

The Luttrell Psalter was prepared for Sir Geoffrey Luttrell, a rich landowner who lived at Irnham in Lincolnshire, in about 1330. Its 309 leaves contain the psalms and canticles in Latin, preceded by a calendar, and followed by a litany with collects and the Office of the Dead with musical notation. It is famous for its decoration, particularly the scenes of everyday life which give us a magnificent – not to say magical – insight into the farming practices of the day. Among the many animals illustrated is a rather emaciated cat playing with a mouse or small rat.

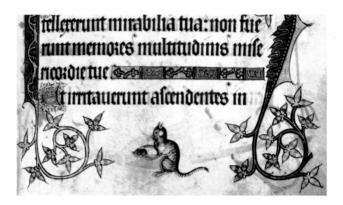

Medieval books of beasts (bestiaries) contain a selection of creatures, both real and imaginary, to which are applied Christian moral and allegorical interpretations. Cats were kept principally for catching mice and rats; their other noteworthy characteristic in this context is their ability to see in the dark. Because of their nocturnal doings, cats came to be linked with witchcraft, the supernatural and, ultimately, Satan himself. From there it was but a step for the cat catching mice to symbolise the devil catching human souls, thus (with false logic) strengthening the view of the cat as personifying Satan.

The spotted, rather weary-looking cat is from a late 12th-century bestiary in Latin; its line drawings continue an English pictorial tradition, with some attempt at accurate representation.

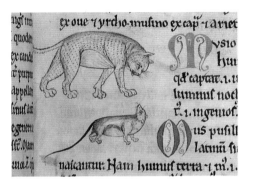

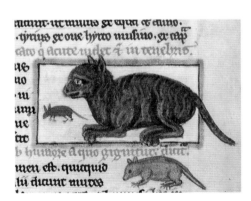

The worried-looking cat – again with the obligatory mouse – is from a bestiary of about 1255, which contains more colour (browns, blues and greens) than the other example.

Leonardo da Vinci

Leonardo da Vinci (1452–1519) drew numerous cat sketches. One of his many fascinations was the study of interlocking curves, so he was particularly interested in the fluidity of the cat. In this work, we can almost see the cat moving – here struggling to get free of little master's arms, there responding to firm stroking – in typical cat–child interactions. These pen-and-ink sketches made in 1478 are associated with larger studies for the *Madonna and Child with Cat.*

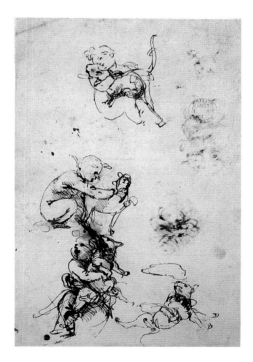

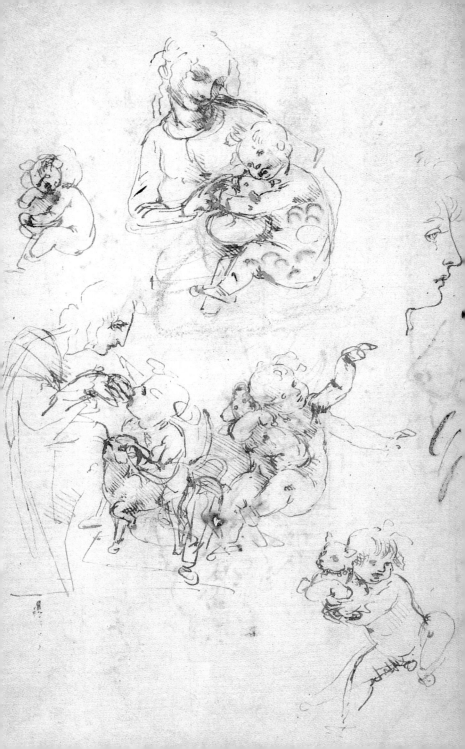

Caxton's

Æsop

William Caxton (1422–91) is notable for having translated and printed the first book in the English language – in Bruges in 1474. He then returned to England and established his own printing press at the Sign of the Red Pale in 1476; his translation of Æsop's *Fables*, with woodcut illustrations, was published in 1484. Æsop is supposed to have flourished in Greece in the 6th century BC. A number of moral tales (fables) featuring animals are attributed to him, as are many more added since. (For further fables, see pages 38 and 46.)

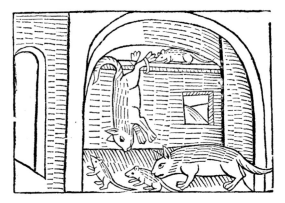

The Catte & the Rat

A cat sought to entice her prey by suspending herself by her hind legs from a peg and pretending to be a bag. But a wise old rat was not fooled: 'Hang there as long as you like, good Madam,' quoth he, 'but I would not come near you, even if you were stuffed with straw'.

thow knowest & wel thyse with thy fayr' face / or euer thow
knowest entryd in to the welle / thow sholest fyrst haue taken
fede/how thow sholdest haue comen out of hit ageyne /
℃ And therfore he whiche is wyse/yf he wysely wylle gouer
ne hym self / ought to take euer good fede to the ende of his
werke

℃ The fourthe fable is of the catte and of the chyken

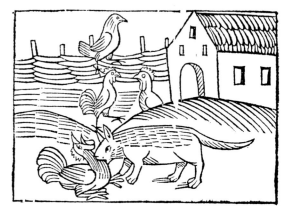

E whiche is fals of kynde/ & hath begonne to trauyle
some other/ euer he wyl vse his craft/ As it apierth
by this present ffable of a kat whiche somtyme toke a
chyken / the whiche he biganne strongly to blame/ for to haue
fonde somme cause that he myght ete hit / and sayd to hym in
this manere / Come hyther thou chyken/ thow dost none other
good but crye alle the nyght/thow letest not the men slepe /
And thenne the chykyn answerd to hym/ I do hit for theyre
grete prouffit / And ouer ageyne the catte sayd to hym/
Yet is there wel wors/ffor thow arte an inceste & lechour

n   iij

The Catte & the Chyken

A cat who took a chicken sought to justify his action,
saying that the chicken was wont to cry 'cock-a-doodle-
doo' all night, and keep people awake. The chicken
replied that he crowed so that people might rise early,
for their greater profit.

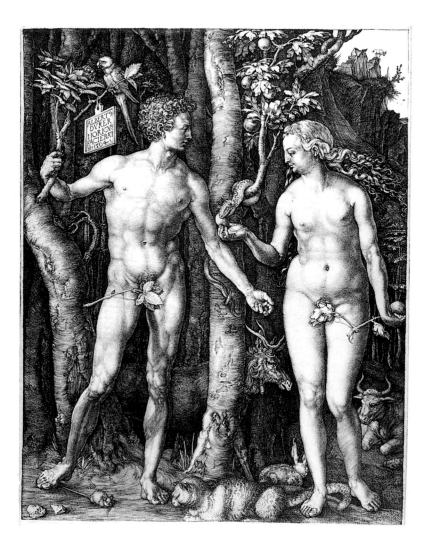

24

Adam

& Eve

The German artist Albrecht Dürer (1471–1528) is well known for his accurate detail and strength of draughtsmanship. The four animals depicted with Adam & Eve (1504) represent (some say) the four temperaments – the melancholic horned beast, the sanguine rabbit, the phlegmatic ox, and the choleric cat – although the temperaments would not come into play until after the Fall. Others suggest that the cat represents the wiles of Eve contemplating the mousy weakness of Adam . . . or vice versa. Or could it just be that Dürer's depiction of the dozing cat, oblivious to the momentous events in the Garden of Eden, is to sum up the essence of the animal?

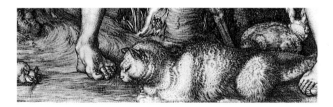

Histories

A cat by an unknown artist in a title page of an edition of the works of Aristotle printed in Venice in 1545. The artist has depicted the cat suckling her kittens standing rather than reclining – indeed, she appears to be dealing with a mouse at the same time. Cats are often depicted with rodents by way of confirming that they *are* cats.

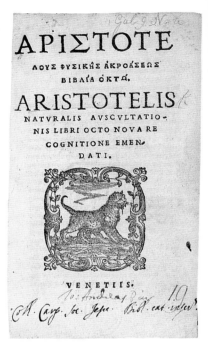

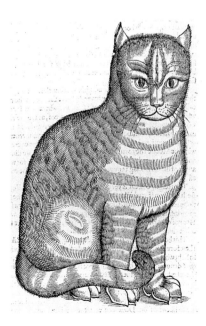

A cat by Edward Topsell (who died about 1638) from *The Historie of Foure-Footed Beasts describing the true and lively Figure of every Beast . . .* (1607). The work draws on an earlier production by Conrad Gesner. This cat is clearly short haired, striped, with an extremely rugged body and robust toes shaped like spades on a playing card – and a disconcertingly human face.

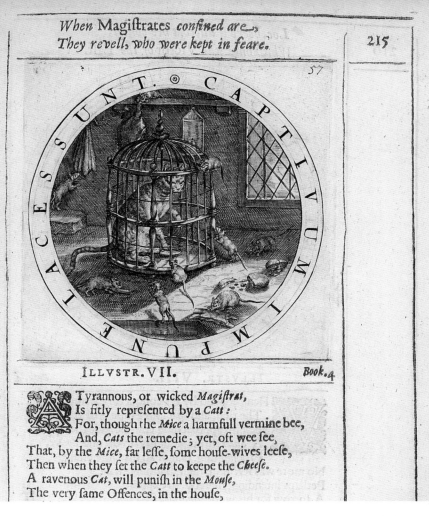

57

ILLVSTR. VII.   *Book. 4.*

Tyrannous, or wicked *Magiftrat,*
Is fitly reprefented by a *Catt :*
For, though the *Mice* a harmfull vermine bee,
And, *Cats* the remedie; yet, oft wee fee,
That, by the *Mice,* far leffe, fome houfe-wives leefe,
Then when they fet the *Catt* to keepe the *Cheefe.*
A ravenous *Cat,* will punifh in the *Moufe,*
The very fame Offences, in the houfe,

George Wither, or Withers (1588–1667), poet, soldier and political satirist, wrote verses in English to accompany the collection of plates published as *Emblemes* in 1635. The plates, then with Greek and Latin inscriptions, had been engraved some twenty years earlier by the Continental artist Crispin Pass. Here, mice besiege a safely-caged cat. As the inscription says – CAPTIVUM IMPUNE LACESSUNT - 'they provoke the prisoner without fear of harm'. At last the mice can play without the cat having to go away.

Witches'
Cats

Some people believed that witches were attended by 'familiars' – supernatural companions who manifested themselves as animals, particularly cats. Old women often kept cats, which of course reinforced the idea that they were witches.

The drawings of witches and their cats on the page opposite were made by Revd Miles Gale (1647–1721), rector of Keighley in Yorkshire, and illustrate Edward Fairfax's account of a witchcraft trial.

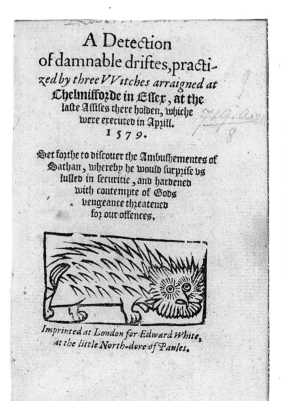

The title page of a book describing the Chelmsford Witchcraft Trials (1579); the animal by an unknown artist is generally thought to be a cat, although the hedgehog and the owl also spring to mind.

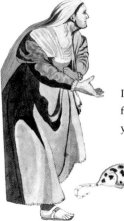

Inges, a white cat spotted with black, is 'the familiar of the witch Margaret Wait the younger'.

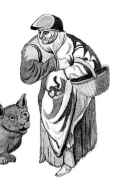

'The great black cat Gibb, which attended Iennet Dibbe for over 40 years.' Gibb was a favourite name for a cat; a gib(b)-cat was one which had been neutered.

A young man named Thomas Forrest 'came riding late near the house of Margaret Wait and there was suddenly assaulted by many cats, so that he could hardly defend himself

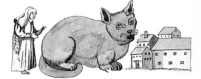

from them; he rode away with all possible speed, and so escaped, though the cats pursued him a long way.'

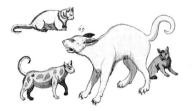

Dick Whittington & His Cat

The real-life Sir Richard Whittington was the son of Sir William Whittington of Gloucestershire; Richard moved to London and prospered as a merchant. He held many high offices and was appointed Lord Mayor of London by King Richard II in 1397. He was re-elected the following year, and again in 1406 and 1419. He lent money to a number of kings of England, and supported many charities. He died in 1423.

At the beginning of the seventeenth century arose the popular tale that a poor boy, Dick Whittington, his only companion a cat, travels to London 'where the streets are paved with gold' to seek his fortune. However, things are not as rosy as he had believed, and he is on the point of turning away when he hears the sound of the bells of London, which seem to say: 'Turn again, Whittington, Lord Mayor of London'.

By good fortune, Dick meets a prosperous merchant, Alderman Fitzwarren, and rids his house of rats by setting Puss on to them. At the same time, the potential for a happy ending is set up when Dick falls in love with the Alderman's beautiful daughter Alice – although at this stage of the story there is no way a poor boy can marry a rich man's daughter.

Fitzwarren is also plagued with rats on one of his merchant ships, so Dick and Puss go off to clear them up and set sail on a voyage to the Mysterious Orient. There, they find that the Sultan's palace is overrun with rats, but Puss comes to the rescue once more. Dick thus reaps a rich reward which enables him, on his return, to secure Alderman Fitzwarren's blessing on his marriage to Alice – and they all live happily ever after; Dick, of course, becomes Sir Richard Whittington, Lord Mayor of London.

There are many versions of this story, which is the basis of one of those peculiarly English entertainments, the pantomime. The 'boy meets unattainable girl and, through a series of adventures, proves himself worthy of her hand in marriage' is a central theme of pantomime. Dick is the 'principal boy' (always played by a girl), and there is plenty of opportunity for introducing Alderman Fitzwarren's comic cook (the 'dame', always played by a man), King Rat (the 'baddie') and his numerous subjects, the jolly captain of the *Saucy Sue* and many more. The role of Puss is simple, but central to the development of the plot; compare it with that of *Puss in Boots* [page 50].

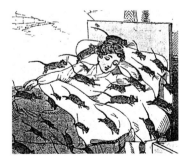

Whittington's attic bedroom, artist unknown (1845).

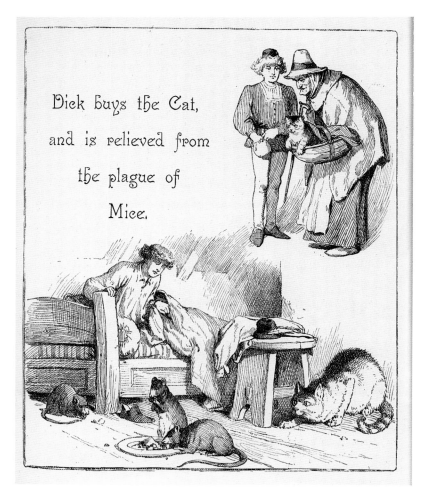

Dick buys the Cat, and is relieved from the plague of Mice.

'Dick buys the Cat and is relieved from the plague of mice';
illustrated by John Proctor (1888). In one version of the story,
Dick does not arrive in London with his cat, but buys a cat
because there are so many rodents in his room. Puss soon
deals with them.

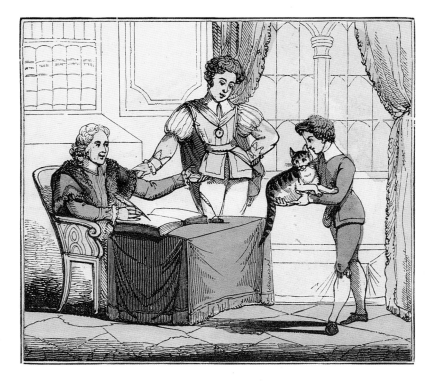

Alderman Fitzwarren is a kind man, and offers all his servants
the chance of sending some possession on his merchant ship to
trade in the East. Dick sends his cat – all that he has.
Artist unknown (1845).

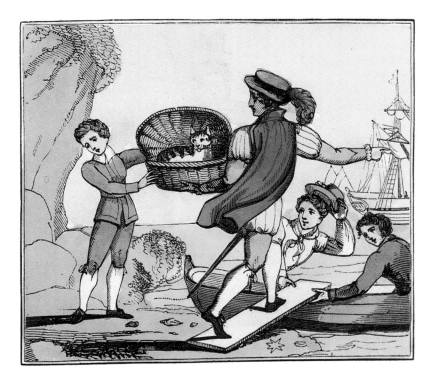

Puss embarks for the journey to the Mysterious Orient. The
sailors in the jolly-boat are pleased to see the cat, because their
ship is overrun with rats. Artist unknown (1845).

Right
The ship has now reached its destination, and the plight of the
Sultan and his wife is revealed. They watch in amazement as
Puss is released to make short work of the rats that have been
plaguing them. Illustration by John Proctor (1888).

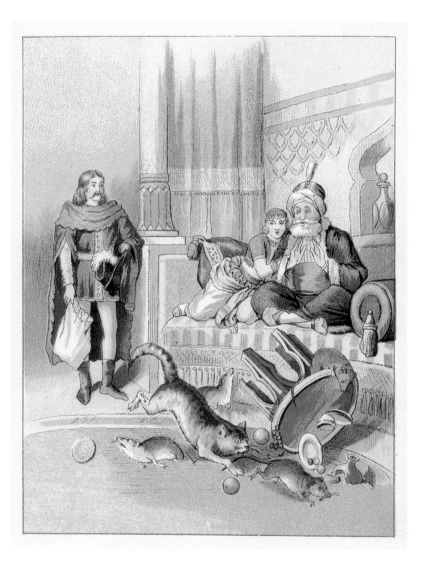

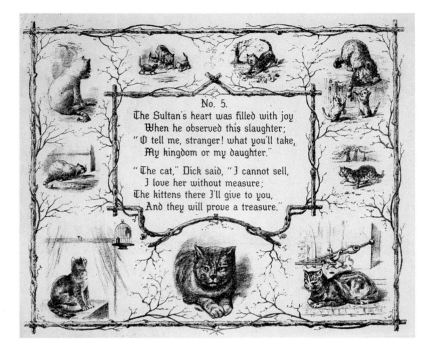

No. 5.

The Sultan's heart was filled with joy
  When he observed this slaughter;
"O tell me, stranger! what you'll take,
  My kingdom or my daughter."

"The cat," Dick said, "I cannot sell,
  I love her without measure;
The kittens there I'll give to you,
  And they will prove a treasure."

The Sultan is so pleased with Puss's success that he offers Dick
a choice: 'The hand of my daughter, or half my kingdom'.
Mindful of Alice at home in London, Dick settles for the half
kingdom. Artist unknown (1874).

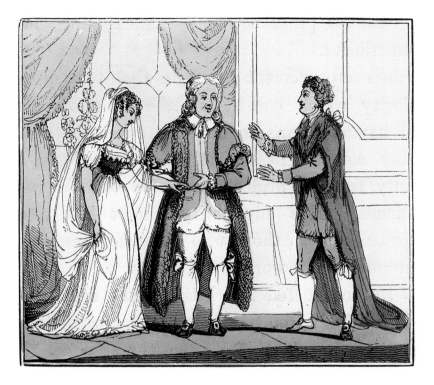

Alice and Dick marry, and they all live happily ever after
– thanks to Puss. Artist unknown (1845).

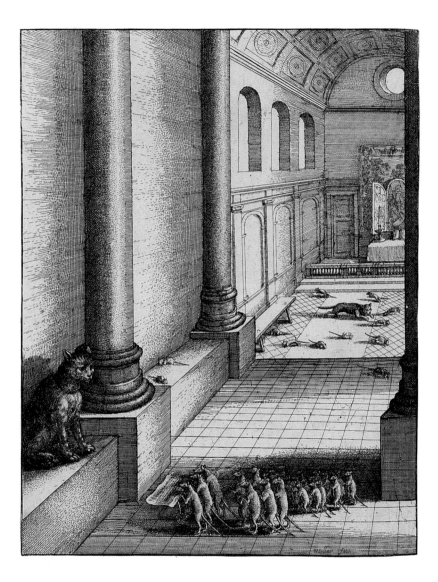

The Cat and the Mice

Wenceslaus Hollar (1707–77) illustrated a number of Æsop's *Fables*. This one, concerning the cat and the mice, is from a book dated about 1751. The cat adopts the monastic life; seeking to ingratiate themselves, the mice bring rich gifts, and the cat invites them to dine. They all march in to the dining hall, whereupon Puss bars the door and massacres them.

Moral:

> 'Treaties are full of Fraud; if rising States
> Would joyn with Princes, and make Kings their Mates,
> Let them beware how they confirm the League;
> Monarchs still jealous for small Cause Renege.'

In the foreground, the mice present a petition; in the background – in another frame of the narrative, as it were – the cat dispatches them.

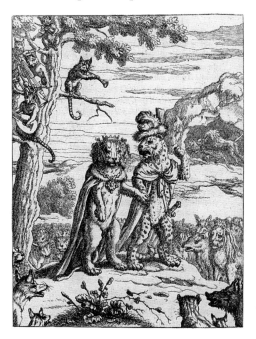

A drawing by an unknown artist in the Hollar volume.

THE

Cats' Concert.

"For regardless at once both of Wind or of Weather,
There were Guests of all sizes and Nations together."

As a boy, William Mulready (1786–1863) became well known for his detailed drawings, and was admitted as a student to the Royal Academy at the age of 14. He produced several little children's books between 1807 and 1809, including *The Cats' Concert* and *Madame Grimalkin's Party*. They were immensely popular in their day, despite the somewhat oppressively detailed drawings, with some of the cats verging on the grotesque. Mulready became a Royal Academician in 1814, and exhibited regularly until his death.

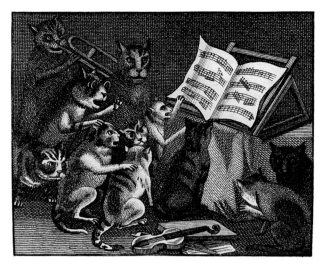

Frontispiece to *The Cats' Concert*; the orchestra seems to be in trouble. The feline musicians are certainly having a worse time than those in the tree on page 39.

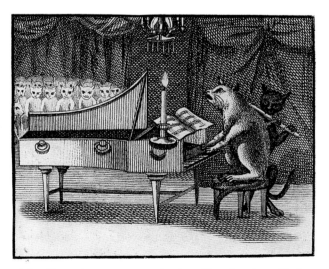

Miss Kitten sings, accompanying herself on the piano; Black Tommy plays the flute.

Le Chat
D'angora

An angora (*ie* Persian) cat, from Jean Baptiste Huet's *Collection des Mammifères du Muséum d'Histoire Naturelle* (1808). One would expect an illustration in such a book to be accurate, but was its face really like that? And what about the position of its tail? Huet made his drawing from a preserved skin, so it might have been difficult to know what it 'really' looked like.

In his commentary, Huet wrote that 'the Angora came originally from Syria, and is much prized for its silky coat. It drinks by lapping with its tongue; when a kitten, it behaves enchantingly. Its claws are normally sheathed, but it uses them for climbing and sometimes for scratching. Its eyes cannot stand bright light. When stroked, the

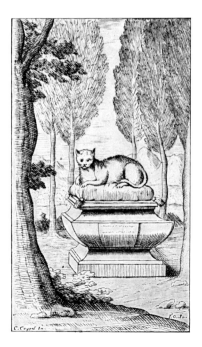

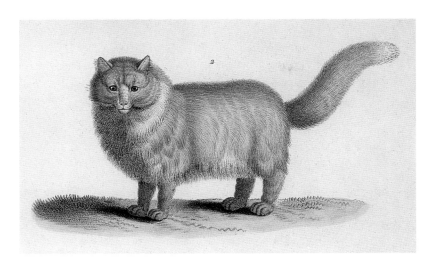

cat's fur generates electricity, especially in frosty weather; you can see sparks in the dark. The Egyptians treated cats as gods, and preserved them with full honours when they died. Even today [1808], some people provide their dead cats with elaborate stone memorials.'

Left Tomb of a cat which belonged to Madame Lesdiguières. Some people have better relationships with animals than they do with their fellow humans, so why should they not erect 'elaborate stone memorials'?

British
Quadrupeds

Edward Donovan (who died in 1837, aged about 65) was a man of private means, which he used to further his studies of the animal kingdom in all its forms. He opened his London Museum & Institute of Natural History to the public in 1807; admission was free. His *Natural History of British Quadrupeds* (1820) illustrates a somewhat spindly domestic cat (below) looking similar to the animal depicted in the Luttrell Psalter [page 18]. His wild cat catching a bird (opposite), on the other hand, looks much more like the domestic cats we know.

How true to life are Donovan's illustrations? A contemporary critic observed that his fishes and insects were good, but that the colouring of the birds and quadrupeds is gaudy, and the drawings of them generally unnatural. His prose also was criticised for its wordiness. Of the domestic cat, he wrote:

'Our common cats, as Linnæus has observed, are very

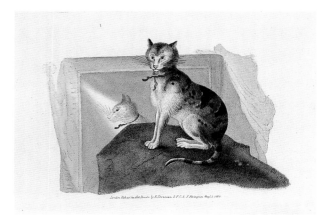

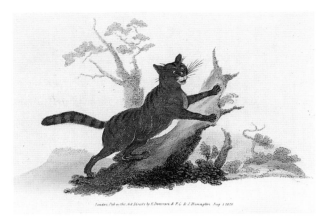

clamorous in their amours. They are particularly con-
tentious when several of the same sex either male or
female meet in their midnight rambles over the house-
tops, out-houses, and gardens; or if a strange cat endeav-
ours to obtain a lodging in a house previously occupied
by one or more, the ire and cruel vengeance of the resi-
dent grimalkins are instantly excited, and the stranger
driven with many bleeding marks of conflict from the
inhospitable roof.

'The merits of this amiable inmate of society are so
universally admitted, that nothing we can offer in praise
of either its intelligence, docility, or use, can tend to place
it in a light more favourable than the reader is already
inclined to view it. Indeed so strongly we are persuaded
must be the prepossession in its behalf, that we may
almost dismiss the subject with observing that the cat pos-
sesses qualities so truly excellent, that her services cannot
be dispensed with.'

Grandville's
La Fontaine

The French author, Jean de La Fontaine (1621–95), derived most of his 239 fables from other sources, notably Æsop and his followers. These 1839 illustrations to his collections are by the caricaturist Grandville (Jean Ignace Isidore Gérard (1803–47)).

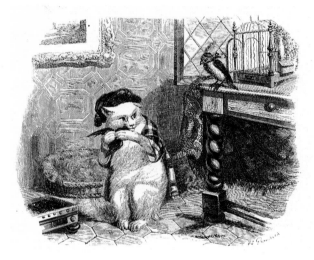

The cat and the two sparrows

A cat lived in the greatest friendship with a sparrow; they had been brought up together since birth. The bird often pecked the cat in fun, but the cat retaliated in jest, with sheathed claws. One day another sparrow came to visit, and the two birds started to argue. 'How dare you insult my friend!' exclaimed puss, and seized and devoured the visitor. Then: 'Really, these sparrows have a most exquisite flavour . . .' She mused upon this until, unable to curtail her desire, she fell upon her friend and ate him.

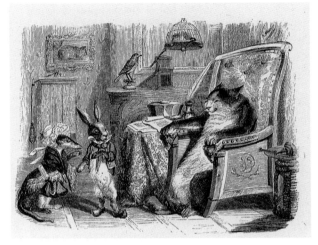

The cat, the weasel and the young rabbit

Master Rabbit went out, and Mistress Weasel moved in to his burrow. Master Rabbit returned: 'What's going on here? Leave at once, or I shall tell all the rats in the kingdom where you are hiding.' Mistress Weasel argued that possession gave her the right to stay – 'But let us refer to Grimalkin and abide by his decision.' They went to speak to the Cat: 'Come nearer my children,' he said, 'for I am somewhat deaf.' They drew nearer, whereupon he darted out his claws in an embrace and devoured both the petitioners. 'This forcibly resembles the justice sometimes dealt out to petty sovereigns, who refer their disputes to more powerful monarchs.'

Compare this fable with Hollar's [page 38].

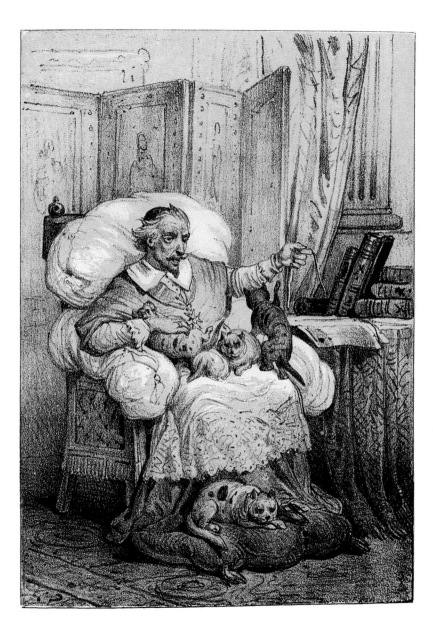

Historic Animals

Otaire Fournier published *Les Animaux Historiques* (*Historic Animals*) in 1845, with illustrations by Victor Adam.

Left A portrait of the powerful French statesman Cardinal Richelieu (1585–1642) playing with his kittens. Richelieu, the real director of French policy throughout most of the reign of King Louis XIII, was not the first to find feline relief from affairs of church and state. It is, perhaps, disappointing to learn that, as soon as his current set of kittens started to grow up and lose their playfulness, the careworn cardinal pensioned them off and sent for some new ones.

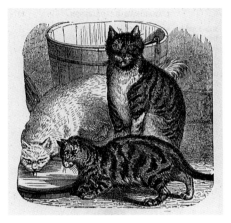

Three Fine Domestic Cats
They look a great deal more cat-like than
some of Richelieu's kittens.

Puss in Boots

There are many editions of the story of *Puss in Boots*, who is an example of the cat as 'the power behind the throne', as we first saw in the story of Dick Whittington [pages 30–37]. An early appearance of Puss in Boots is in *Piacevoli Notti* (*Pleasant Nights*) (1550–3), by Giovan Francesco Straparola who died in about 1577. In 1697, Charles Perrault (1528–1703) published *Histoires ou contes du temps passé, avec des moralités (Histories & tales of long ago, with morals),* based on traditional folk tales, in which the story appears as *Le Maitre Chat ou Le Chat Botté*, which was translated into English by Robert Samber as *Puss in Boots* (1729) and has been retold many times with illustrations by many illustrators. It also makes a fine pantomime [see page 31], as it has such a beautifully-crafted plot.

The old miller dies; his first son inherits the mill, his second the donkey, and his third the cat – to the amusement of his brothers – but it turns out to be no ordinary cat, and contrives to make his master a prince by arranging for him to marry the King's daughter. Puss begins by asking his master for a pair of boots and a sack. He catches some rabbits in the sack, and takes them to the King: 'a present from my master, the Marquis of Carabas' (Puss's invention). The King is duly impressed. Puss takes further gifts to the King, whose admiration for the Marquis grows.

When Puss hears that the King is to go on a tour, he sends his master bathing, and hides his clothes. Along comes the carriage bearing the King and his daughter. 'Help, help,' cries Puss, 'my master, the Marquis of Carabas, is drowning – some robbers stole his clothes and threw him in the water.'

Recalling the gifts of game, the King stops the coach and commands that the Marquis should be rescued and clothed – after which, of course, he looks every inch a nobleman. The Marquis enters the coach and they drive on, Puss running ahead and priming the reapers in the fields to say that the crops belong to 'the Marquis of Carabas'.

A wicked ogre has been causing havoc in the land, and Puss boldly visits him in his castle. Puss flatters the ogre into demonstrating his magical powers, persuading him to turn into a mouse – which Puss then dispatches. Puss now has possession of the ogre's castle, complete with the banquet the ogre was about to eat, and is able to welcome the royal coach to the 'Marquis's Palace'.

By now, the King is so impressed that there is no bar to his daughter marrying the Marquis of Carabas, whom he creates a Prince – and all thanks to Puss.

Some critics were concerned at the plot of *Puss in Boots*; the illustrator George Cruikshank, for example, found the tale 'quite unfit for the young', and rewrote it so that the 'poor boy' was really a prince ousted by the ogre, and the cat a metamorphosed gamekeeper. Cruikshank had already turned the children's tales *Hop-o-my-Thumb* and

Cinderella into temperance tracts; no wonder Charles Dickens described his behaviour as 'a fraud on the fairies' and 'the intrusion of a whole hog of unwieldy dimensions into the fairy flower-garden'. The master-cat probably never made any child a rogue, even though his conduct was flagrantly immoral.

Compare the role of the cat in *Puss in Boots* with that in *Dick Whittington*. Dick Whittington's cat does what a cat (of those days) should do – catch rats. Puss's rat-catching prowess is the foundation of his master's success. Puss in Boots, however, is proactive; he maps out the path for his master's success, and causes things to happen. His approach is very different from that of Whittington's Puss.

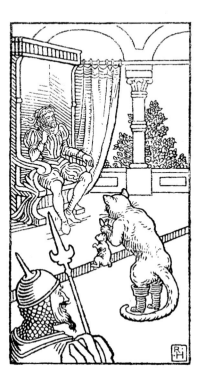

Puss presents a plump rabbit to the King; R Heighway's 1895 version.

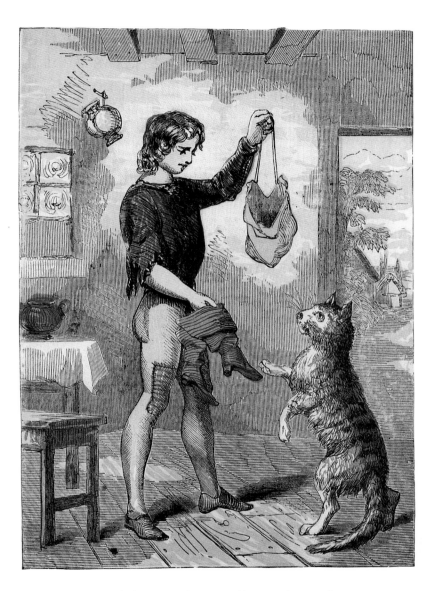

Puss asks his master for a pair of boots and a game bag.
Artist unknown (1858).

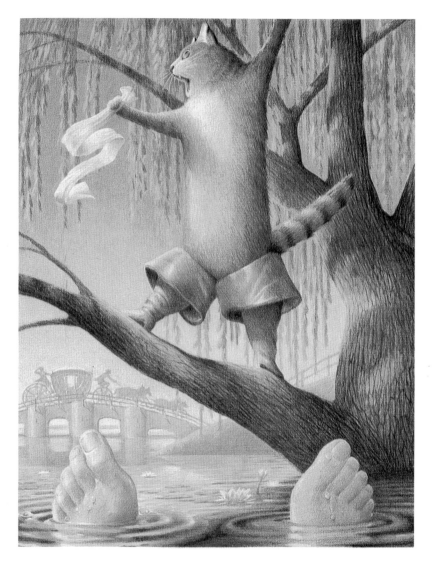

'Help! Help! My master, the Marquis of Carabas is drowning!'
From the American artist Fred Marcellino's much-admired
Puss in Boots (1991).

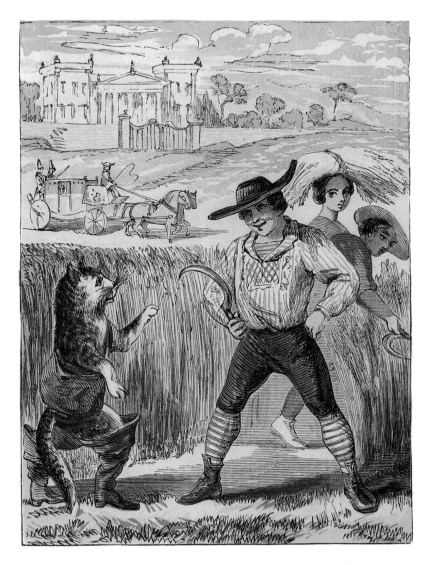

'If anyone asks you to whom these lands belong, answer, they belong to the Lord Marquis of Carabas.' His master safely dressed and in the coach, Puss runs ahead to prime the reapers. Artist unknown (1858).

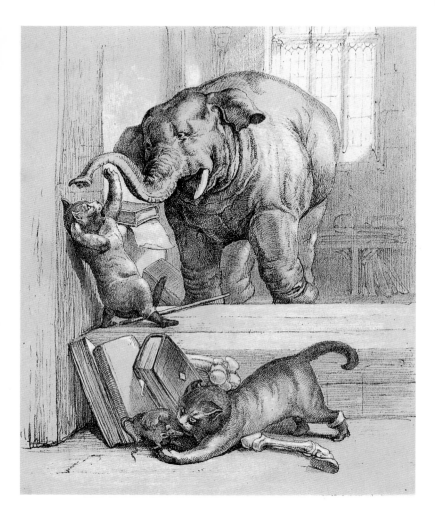

In Otto Speckter's drawing (1844), Puss tricks the ogre into turning first into an elephant, then into a mouse – whereupon he kills and devours him.

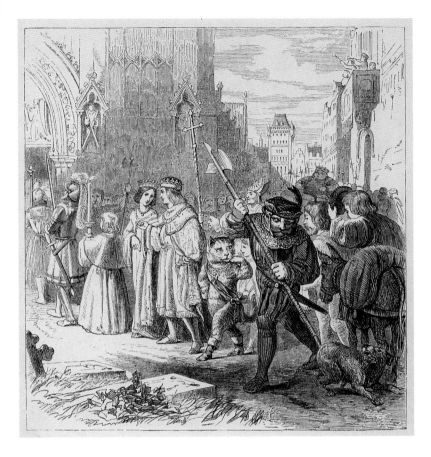

In a later Otto Spekter drawing (1856) the Marquis of Carabas marries and becomes a prince; Puss is made prime minister.

The White Cat

The White Cat (1847; illustrated by 'JW') is a translation from one of the first collections to be described as 'fairy tales' (*Contes des Fées*) published by the prolific French writer Marie Catherine La Mothe, Countess d'Aulnoy, in three volumes in 1698.

A king had three sons. To find out who should inherit the throne, he sent them off saying that the one who brought him the most perfect little dog would be his successor. The youngest set out and came to a wonderful palace where disembodied hands guided him to the beautiful but mournful White Cat. Hearing his story, the White Cat gave him an acorn to take home to his brothers and the King. Inside the acorn was the most perfect little dog!

Then the King sent the three off for a piece of cambric fine enough to pass through the eye of a needle. The youngest prince visited the White Cat again, and she gave him the requisite piece of cambric.

The King sets a third task: to find the most beautiful woman, worthy of becoming a princess. Now the White Cat commands the prince to cut off her head and tail; when he finally brings himself to do this, she turns into a beautiful princess with six kingdoms of her own. The King keeps his kingdom, she gives one of hers to each of the elder brothers, and she and her prince rule the other four.

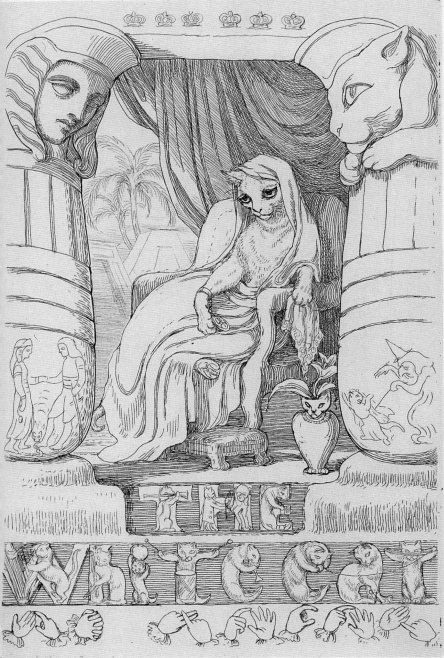

Drawn & Lith by J.W.

Publ. by Wm. Blackwood & Sons. Edinburgh & London.

Struwwelpeter

Heinrich Hoffmann-Donner (1809–1894), a doctor of medicine, took to drawing in order to divert his youthful patients; his first collection of illustrated cautionary tales was published in Germany in 1845. *The English Struwwelpeter* (*Shock-headed Peter*), appeared in 1848, and various versions have been in print ever since.

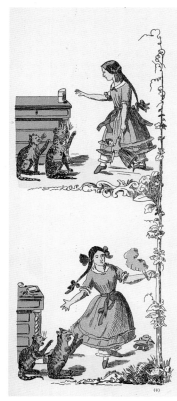

Pauletta's parents both went out,
So quite alone she played about.
She jumped and sang with all her might,
And dolly gave her great delight;
When suddenly, see, what a prize!
A pretty match-box caught her eyes.
"Oh! what a lovely toy you 'll make!"
She said, and went the box to take;—
"I 'll strike a match, 't will be such fun;
I know exactly how it 's done."

But Tib and Tab, the danger seeing,
To stop Pauletta both agreeing,
Held up their paws and warned her, saying:
"Papa forbids this sort of playing;
Stop it! miaow!" each cried in turn,
"Or else you 'll like a bonfire burn."

To this Pauletta listen'd not;
The match she struck burnt bright and hot,
It gave off sparks, and smoke, and flame,
The picture shows just how they came.
Pauletta this delightful found,
And skipped with pleasure round and round.

But Tib and Tab, the danger seeing,
To stop Pauletta both agreeing,
Held up their paws and warned her, saying:
"Mamma forbids this sort of playing;
Drop it! miaow!" each cried in turn,
"Or else you 'll like a bonfire burn."

(6)

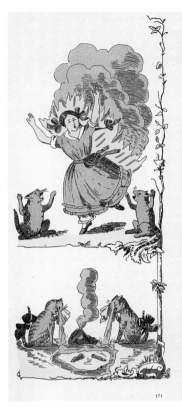

Alas! her dress has caught on fire,
The cruel flames rise high—rise higher!
They burn her hand! they burn her hair!
Alas! they burn her ev'rywhere!

Poor Tib and Tab for help are seeking,
And both at once are sadly shrieking.
"Come quick! come quick!" they loudly cry
"Or else the flaming child will die!
Mee-o! miaow! mee-o! miaow!
She's burning like a bonfire now!"

Now all is burnt with flames and smoke,
Pauletta's but a heap of coke,
Though still her pretty shoes remain,
To tell a tale of dreadful pain.

Now sitting where the shoes are lying,
Both Tib and Tab for grief are crying:
"Miaow! me-ew! miaow! me-ew!
Unhappy parents, where are you?"
Like little brooks, through meadows going
Upon the ground their tears are flowing.

(7)

Pauletta and the Matches is the same story as the better-
known Harriet and the Matches, but the verse is different (and the illustrations slightly different).

Harrison Weir

1851 was the year of the Great Exhibition, when Joseph Paxton's Crystal Palace was built in Hyde Park, London. Among the many highly-acclaimed exhibits from the world over were *tableaux* of stuffed animals set up by Hermann Ploucquet, Preserver of Objects of Natural History at the Royal Museum of Stuttgart (the capital of the kingdom of Wurtemberg). And among 'The Comical Creatures of Wurtemberg' was a *tableau* of cats, although as shown they have a somewhat stoat-like appearance. Was this an accurate representation of the cats of Wurtemberg, or the product of the taxidermist's fancy? The exhibit was so popular that a little book was published showing the *tableaux* with accompanying stories.

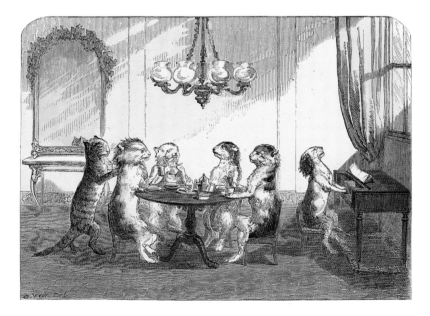

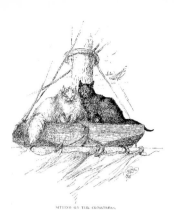

SITTING ON THE CROSSTREES.

This illustration, in Weir's typical pen-and-ink style, is from *Shireen and her Friends – Pages from the Life of a Persian Cat* by Gordon Stables (1895).

A domestic cat from *The Pleasure Book of Domestic Animals* (1865).

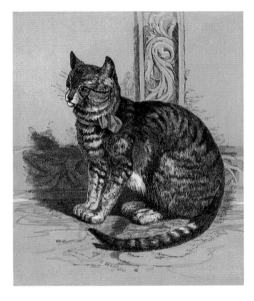

Left The Comical Creatures of Wurtemberg: 'The Kittens at Tea – Miss Paulina singing'. The drawing is signed H Weir, an early example of the work of Harrison William Weir (1824–1906), an artist later famous for his animal drawings, and his tireless championing of the cat. Weir was responsible for the first Cat Show at the Crystal Palace in 1871 and for the foundation of the National Cat Club.

Dame Trot

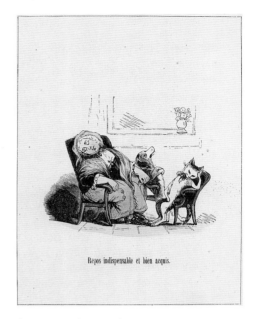

Repos indispensable et bien acquis.

Dame Trot and her Wonderful (or Comical) Cat was a favourite nursery tale throughout the 19th century. There were many different versions; the book illustrated by Will Gibbons (1888) opens:

Dame Trot came home one wintry night
A shivering starving soul,
But Puss had made a blazing fire
And nicely trussed a fowl.

Next morning Puss got up betimes,
The Breakfast cloth she laid;
And, ere the village clock struck VIII,
The TEA and TOAST she made.

They enjoy the meal, and open a bottle of wine. 'The wine got up in Pussy's head', and caused her to dance, and attempt to ride on Spot the dog, much to Dame Trot's amusement. They all fell asleep, but Puss was up bright and early to make breakfast.

The Dame goes out, and Puss and Spot play cards; then Puss plays her flute and teaches Spot to dance.

These are just some of their antics, illustrated here. Puss making toast is a Gibbons illustration; the other three are from a French edition of 1858.

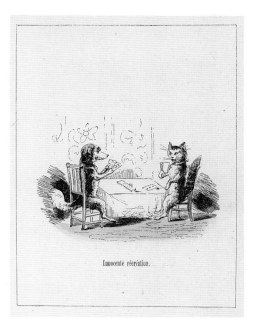

Innocente récréation.

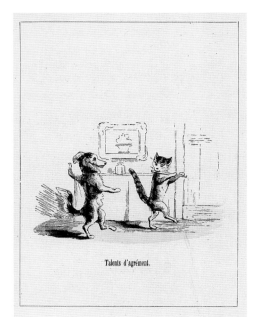

Talents d'agrément.

In the Middle Ages, qualified women in the kingdom of Naples were allowed to practise surgery and gynaecology. One of the best-known 12th-century treatises on obstetrics is by Dame Trotula (or Trot) of Salerno. Was she the inspiration for the Dame with the Comical Cat?

The Cheshire Cat

Here is the Cheshire cat as depicted by Sir John Tenniel in Lewis Carroll's *Alice's Adventures in Wonderland* (1865). The cat first appears in the Duchess's kitchen:

'Please would you tell me,' said Alice . . . 'why your cat grins like that?'

'It's a Cheshire cat' said the Duchess, 'and that's why.' Later Alice said to the Cat: '. . . I wish you wouldn't keep appearing and vanishing so suddenly: you make one quite giddy!'

All right,' said the Cat; and this time it vanished quite slowly, beginning with the end of the tail, and ending with the grin, which remained some time after the rest of it had gone.

The phrase 'Grinning like a Cheshire cat' predated (and hence presumably inspired) Carroll's creation. Its origin is uncertain, but may lie in the grinning-lion creations of a particular Cheshire inn-sign painter, or the tradition of fashioning Cheshire cheeses in the shape of grinning cats – possibly to commemorate the famous angry grin of the 14th-century John Catherall who died defending the City of Chester. Carroll (Charles L Dodgson, 1832–98) was born in Daresbury, Cheshire; a commemorative window in Daresbury Church dedicated in 1934 features a Cheshire Cat.

The original story was entitled *Alice's Adventures Underground*, handwritten and illustrated by Carroll; unfortunately, it omits the Cheshire Cat altogether. When preparing the book for publication, Carroll invited

"Well, then," the Cat went on, "you see a dog growls when it's angry, and wags its tail when it's pleased. Now *I* growl when I'm pleased, and wag my tail when I'm angry. Therefore I'm mad."

"*I* call it purring, not growling," said Alice.

"Call it what you like," said the Cat. "Do you play croquet with the Queen to-day?"

Tenniel to illustrate it. The project was a stormy one, with Carroll accepting only one of Tenniel's pictures without modification. Nevertheless, Tenniel's pictures have become the standard, and it requires an open mind to accept others.

Arthur Rackham (1867–1939) illustrated Alice in 1907 (opposite). Rackham had a talent for depicting the make-believe world in a complex and sinister manner comparable with Richard Dadd's fairy scenes, or W Heath Robinson's serious work. The general aura of gloom is heightened by his use of sombre colours, and the implication that there is more going on than meets the eye.

Harry Rountree (1878–1950) was born in New Zealand and arrived in London in 1901 with his portfolio of animal drawings and an introduction to an editor. The obvi-

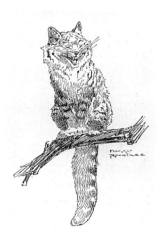

ously jaded editor advised him to go back to New Zealand; fortunately, he chose to stay on and became one of the foremost animal artists of his time, working in both humorous and serious styles. His Cheshire Cat (left) appeared in 1928.

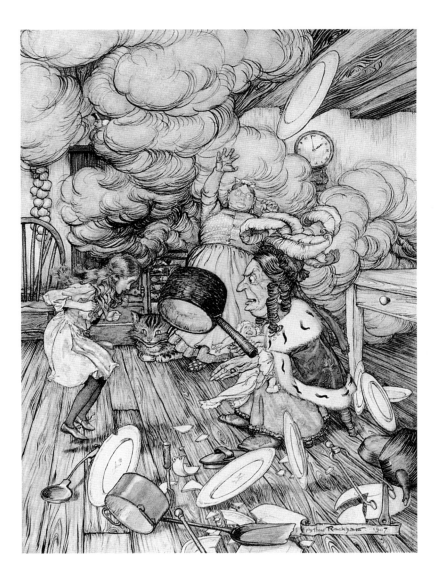

Edward Lear

Edward Lear (1812–88), zoological draughts-man, traveller, landscape painter, and drawing master to Queen Victoria, is widely remembered for his nonsense verse. The popularity of his enormous tabby [Old] Foss (1870– 87) was part of the late-19th-Century rise

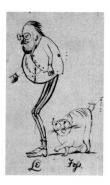

of interest in the domestic cat. Here, Foss is depicted in the heraldic terms of the noble lion: 'couchant' (in repose), 'regardant' (looking at the spectator), 'rampant' (on hind legs), and 'passant' (walking); and in pseudo-heraldic terms: 'a untin', 'dansant', and 'pprpr' (a pun on the heraldic 'proper' *ie* in natural colours).

From 1871 until his death, Lear lived in San Remo; when he moved to a new house, he had it built to the same plan as the old one so that Foss would not be disconcerted. In due time, Foss was buried in the garden with a suitably inscribed head-stone.

In his poem 'How pleasant to know Mr Lear', we find:

> He has many friends, laymen and clerical;
> Old Foss is the name of his cat;
> His body is perfectly spherical,
> He weareth a runcible hat.

The sketch at the end of a letter from Lear dated 16 June 1884 clearly shows the two-year-old Foss; unfortunately, Mr Lear is not wearing a runcible hat.

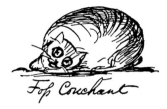

Fos Couchant

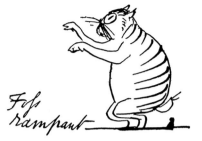

Fos rampant

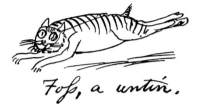

Fos, a untin.

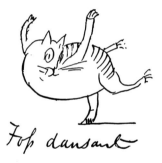

Fos dansant

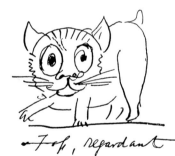

Fos, regardant

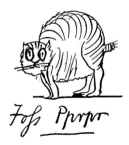

Fos Pprpr

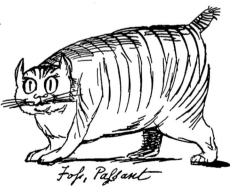

Fos, Passant

The Owl and the Pussycat

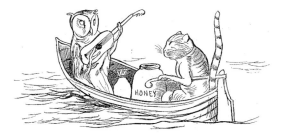

Edward Lear's *The Owl and the Pussycat* (1871) are well known for going to sea in their beautiful pea-green boat.

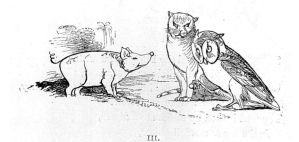

III.

Having agreed to marry, the Owl and the Pussycat buy a ring from a Piggy-wig.

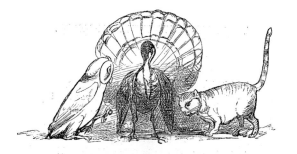

The Turkey (who lives on the hill) performs the wedding ceremony.

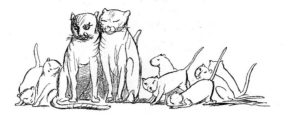

'There was a Family of Two old Cats and Seven young
Cats . . .' from *The History of the Seven Families.*

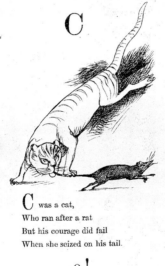

C

C was a cat,
Who ran after a rat
But his courage did fail
When she seized on his tail.

c !

Crafty old Cat !

From a *Nonsense Alphabet*

Victorian children's illustrations

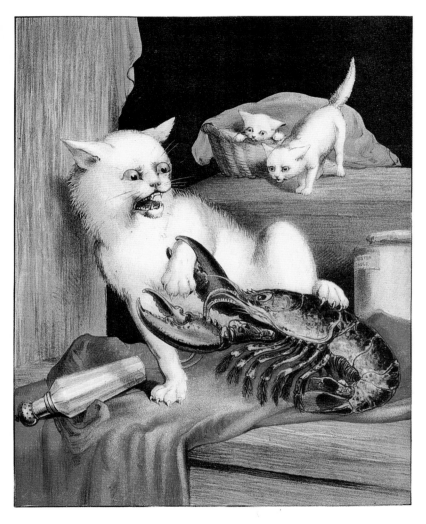

Pussies at Mischief: Meg & the Lobster. Artist unknown (1873).

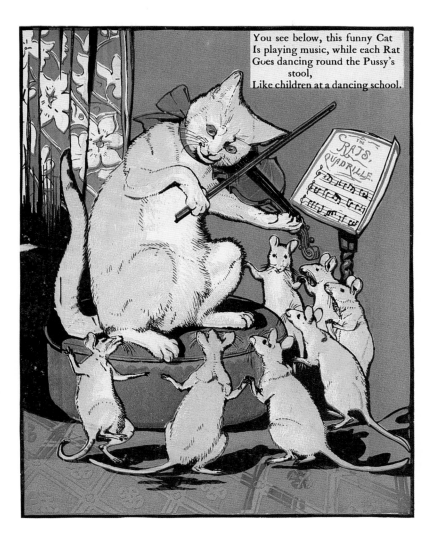

Pussie Cat's ABC book. Artist unknown (1880).

The House that Jack Built

Randolph Caldecott (1846–1886) joined a bank at the age of 15. He studied at the Manchester School of Art in his spare time, and built up a reputation as an artist which enabled him to resign from the bank in 1872. From then on his work was in enormous demand. In 1878 he was invited to illustrate two children's books: *The House that Jack Built* and *John Gilpin*. He continued to publish two children's books each year for the next seven years. The whole series was immensely popular, and sold over one million copies. Caldecott died at the age of 40 in Florida, whence he had gone for the good of his health.

The House that Jack Built is a 'cumulative rhyme'; it begins: 'This is the house that Jack built', and builds up line by line until it reaches:

This is the Farmer sowing his corn

That kept the Cock that crowed in the morn

That waked the Priest all shaven and shorn

That married the Man all tattered and torn

That kissed the Maiden all folorn

That milked the Cow with the crumpled horn

That tossed the Dog

That worried the Cat

That killed the Rat

That ate the Malt

That lay in the House that Jack built.

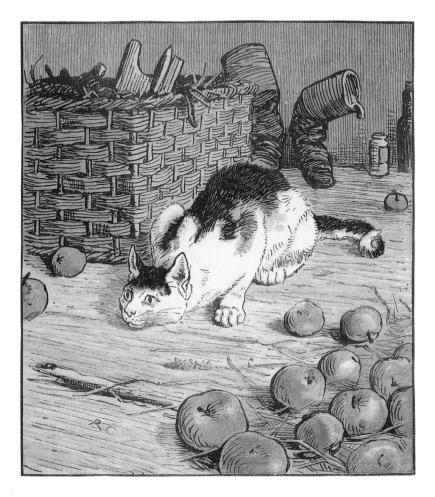

Caldecott's treatment of the cat, with its beautifully-observed curling tail, has a Japanese air about it.

Louis Wain

Louis William Wain (1860–1939) was a popular artist whose name became synonymous with comical cats. HG Wells said (1927): 'He has made the cat his own. He invented a cat style, a cat society, a whole cat world. English cats that do not look and live like Louis Wain cats are ashamed of themselves.' Wain played an important part in promoting the cause of the cat, and was the (somewhat eccentric) President of the National Cat Club from 1891. He was admitted to the pauper ward of a mental hospital in 1924. The following year, he was 'discovered' there, a fund was raised for his welfare, and he was transferred to the comparative comfort of Bethlem Royal Hospital, and later Napsbury Hospital, near St Albans, where he ended his days, drawing to the last.

The early narrative sequence *Our Cats – a Domestic History* [page 81] appeared in the *Illustrated London News* in 1884. Wain's early style is similar to that of his friend Harrison Weir [page 62], perhaps a consequence of drawing for line reproduction. The Louis Wain cat began to emerge about 1890; in the next 20 years he illustrated over 100 books – half his lifetime's output – as well as contributing numerous drawings to periodicals for both children and adults.

Opposite and overleaf Just three of the hundreds of postcards Louis Wain designed in the 1900s. He could have become an extremely rich man, but he never had an agent, and always sold the rights in his work.

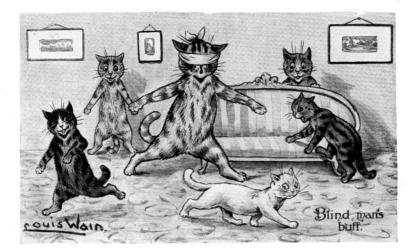

Blind man's buff.

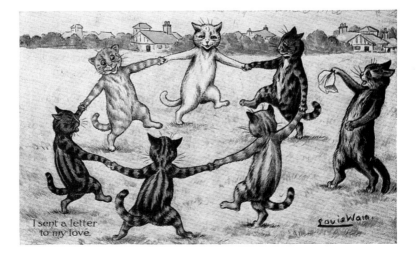

I sent a letter to my love.

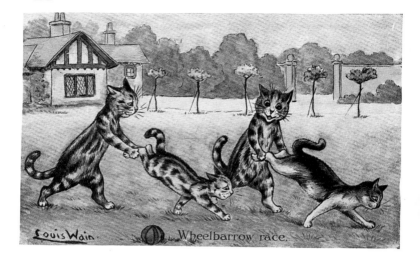

Our Cats – a Domestic History *(opposite)*

1 The family goes to the seaside: Miss Clara's pet is forgotten.

2 The Cat, left behind, diverts herself with the sparrows.

3 Commits larceny at the milk-cans.

4 Helps herself at the cats'-meat basket.

5 Looks sharp after the mice.

6 But they keep out of danger (and this Cat becomes so thin, that she is not fit to be sent to the Cat Show).

7 On the contrary, the Jones's Cat, which has not been so neglected, arrives in good condition at the Crystal Palace.

8 & 9 She plays and enjoys herself.

10 Eats well. 11 Drinks. 12 Cleans herself.

13 Rests and sleeps.

14 Returns home, crowned with honours.

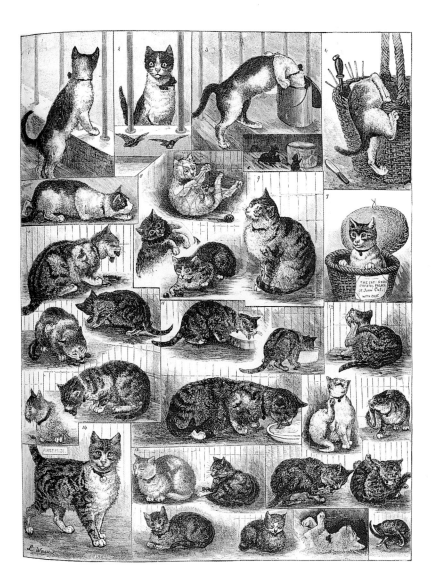

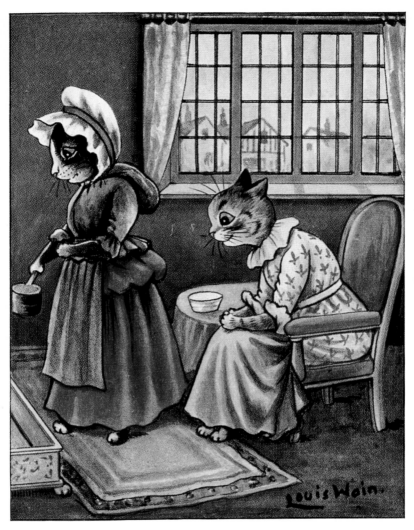

The Tale of Little Priscilla Purr (1920) was an attempt by the publisher Valentine to compete with the Beatrix Potter publications [page 90]. The book (and its three companion volumes) are the same size and layout as Potter's, but neither the text nor the illustrations gets anywhere near Potter's charm.

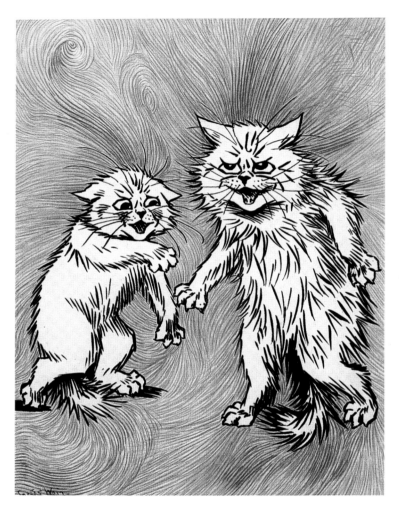

The Fire of the Mind Agitates the Atmosphere (1930s)

Powerful brown swirls emanate from the cats like the lines of force from magnets, made visible by means of iron filings. The cat on the left seems to be exercising an evil influence upon the cat on the right. Perhaps this was a reflection of Wain's view of the world – that his body was charged with electricity, and that ether – the source of all evil – was present in his food.

Henriette Ronner

Madame Ronner (1821–1902) was born in Amsterdam, and spent a lifetime supporting her invalid husband and family by portraiture and animal painting. It was later in life that she came to concentrate on the studies of cats and kittens for which she became famous. She worked fast, composing her subjects in terms of light and shade rather than as forms separated by lines. This enabled her to capture 'their quiet dignity as they repose superbly on their luxurious cushions, immersed in sober thought; the piquant look of surprise in the large-eyed kittens; their comical helplessness in doze and slumber – these have been obtained only by intimate knowledge grafted on to high artistic power.'

This picture of Madame Ronner at work (1894) shows how 'her sitters are detained comfortably reclining upon cushions in their glass cage'. In an interview the following year, Louis Wain [page 78] said: 'Cats are most difficult things to sketch unless they are put under a glass case with a nice cosy nest inside it, for they seem to get restless and uncomfortable when they see anyone looking hard at them and moving a pencil.' The thought came from Madame Ronner (whom he admired) but it is doubtful if Wain ever used the technique.

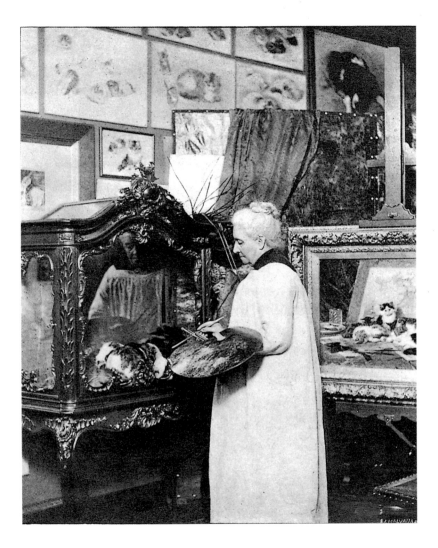

The Black
Cat

'The Black Cat' *(right)* by Aubrey Beardsley (1872–98). Edgar Allan Poe (1809–49) included 'The Black Cat' in his *Tales of the Grotesque and Arabesque* (1840). After a series of nastinesses, the protagonist murders his wife and walls up her body, but does not notice that the black cat contrives to join his late mistress. Eventually, the police hear the crying of the cat, and tear down the wall: sitting upon the head of the corpse, 'with red extended mouth and solitary eye of fire, sat the hideous beast whose craft had seduced me into murder, and whose informing voice had consigned me to the hangman. I had walled the monster up within the tomb!'

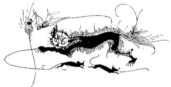

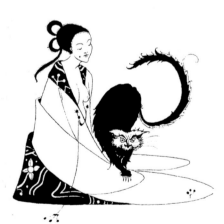

Vignettes drawn by Beardsley for Smith & Sheridan's *Bon Mots*. The representations of the finely-observed cats are typical of Beardsley's mastery of complementary black and white forms.

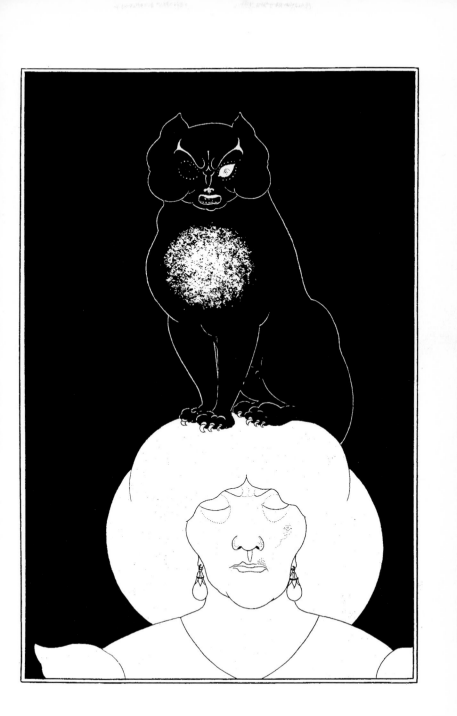

The Cat that Walked by Himself

Rudyard Kipling (1865–1936) illustrated his own *Just-So Stories* (1902) – imaginative children's tales of the earliest times when (according to Kipling) things came to be as they are now.

In the story of 'The Cat that Walked by Himself', Man meets Woman; they move into a cave and set up the first household. Dog, Horse and Cow come out of the Wild Woods, approach the cave, and become domesticated. But Cat said: 'I am not a friend, and I am not a servant. I am the Cat who walks by himself, and all places are alike to me.' Woman made a bargain with him: if she spoke three words in his praise he could enter the cave, sit by the fire, and drink milk. Baby arrives; Cat amuses Baby, and sends him to sleep, and catches a mouse, thus securing the three words of praise.

Cat keeps his side of the bargain: he is kind to babies (as long as they don't pull his tail too hard) and he keeps the mice down. But when night comes, he is once again the Cat that walks by himself.

Of his illustration, Kipling wrote: 'This is the picture of the Cat that Walked by Himself, walking by his wild lone through the Wet Wild Woods and waving his wild tail.' Kipling's perspective conveys a feeling of immense loneliness.

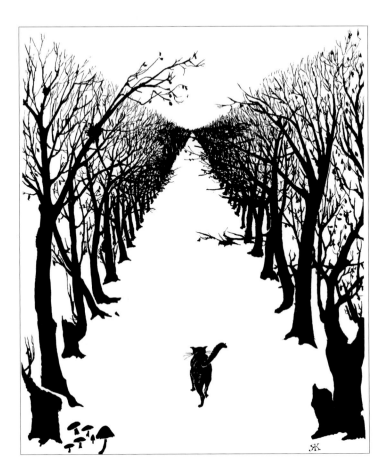

Tom Kitten
&
The Roly-Poly
Pudding

Beatrix Potter was a fine, self-taught draughtsman, who wrote and illustrated *The Tale of Peter Rabbit* in the time-honoured way – for a young friend – in 1893. After its publication in 1902, a score of tales in similar vein followed, though her marriage in 1913 marked the end of her most prolific period. Beatrix Potter was one of the first writer–illustrators to make the interchange between the real world and the story-book cat seem plausible. *The Tale of Tom Kitten* was published in 1907, and the following year Tom featured in *The Roly-Poly Pudding* (later *The Tale of Samuel Whiskers*).

'Once upon a time there was an old cat, called Mrs Tabitha Twitchit , who was an anxious parent.' One baking day, her son Tom was nowhere to be found – he didn't want to be shut in a cupboard like his sisters! In fact, he had climbed the chimney in the old house – modelled on the artist's house at Sawrey in the English Lake District, and to be seen to this day – and found himself lost in the stonework. 'All at once, he fell head over heels in the dark, down a hole, and landed on a heap of very dirty rags' at the feet of the old rat Samuel Whiskers. Samuel and his wife Anna Maria truss up Tom Kitten, and go down to the kitchen of the house to steal some dough and a rolling pin to make Tom into a roly-poly pudding. But Mrs Twitchit and Cousin Ribby hear the roly-poly noise under the floor, and send John Joiner in to investigate. Tom is saved, and the rats pack up and leave the house. Tom's mother and Cousin Ribby strip off the dough, and make it into a bag pudding 'with currants in it to hide the smuts'.

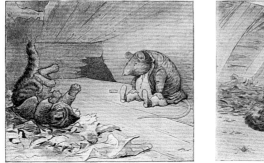

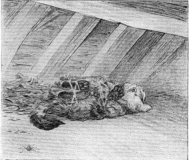

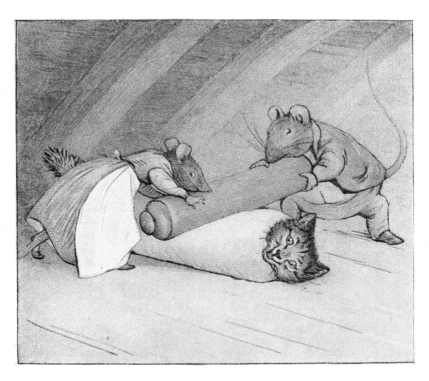

Cecil
Aldin

Cecil Aldin (1870–1935) began to draw for the press in 1891. He quickly became known for his style of animal drawing, and illustrated many books. He was more prolific with dogs than with cats; *The White Kitten Book* (1909) is a rare example of his cat illustration.

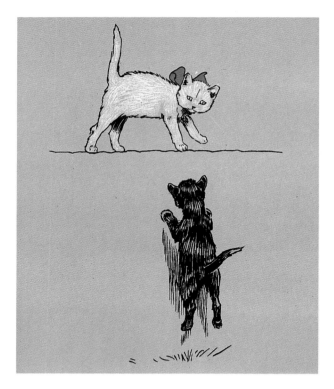

Harry Whittier Freese

In the 1930s, the American Harry Whittier Freese made a speciality of photographing *tableaux* of kittens dressed up and arranged with crude props. *Four Little Kittens* (1934) is 'Dedicated to all the little kittens who posed for the pictures in this book'. A note reads: 'These unusual photographs of real kittens were made possible only by patient, unfailing kindness on the part of the photographer at all times.' The implication is that the photographer used live kittens, but it is difficult to know for sure. The same photographs were later used with different (rhyming) text.

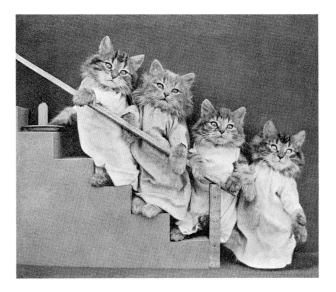

Krazy Kat

George Herriman (1880–1944) began drawing comic strips in 1901. By 1921, he had settled in Hollywood, and was working exclusively for Hearst Newspapers.

Krazy Kat – of Coconino County in the Arizona Desert – evolved from a minor character in an early Herriman cartoon *The Family Upstairs*. He escaped to star in his own comic strip in about 1913, and until 1944 enhanced Hearst's *City Life* week-end supplements, 'designed to appeal to intellectual readers who were otherwise revulsed by the scandals on the front page.'

We who are saturated with the cleverness and electronic wizardry of modern cartoons benefit from studying Herriman's innovations. In this strip of 1935, Krazy Kat finds a number of uses for a tortilla (or 'toteeya'). We can begin to savour the idiosyncratic spelling and phraseology; on closer examination, we appreciate the subplot of the mouse with the brick; then it dawns on us that, while the characters stay in one place, the landscape changes around them – indeed, the landscape is one of the characters. This example was one of the first Krazy Kat strips to move into the colour section, and colour gave Herriman yet another medium for experiment.

Like all great art, Krazy Kat is less simple than it first appears. It demands study, but that study is well worth the effort, and we begin to see why so many cartoon aficionados regard Krazy Kat as the greatest ever.

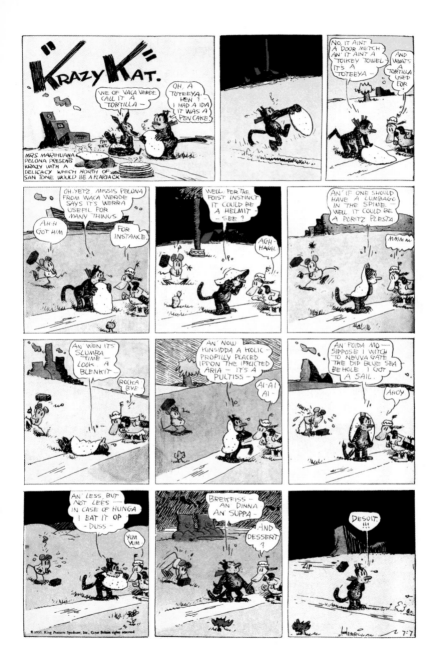

95

Orlando, The Marmalade Cat

Kathleen Hale introduced *Orlando, the Marmalade Cat* in 1938. 'Orlando was very beautiful, striped like marmalade and the same colour; his eyes reminded you of twin green gooseberries. He and his dear wife Grace had three kittens – the Tortoiseshell Pansy, snow-white Blanche and coal-black Tinkle.'

The 18 tales of Orlando and his family have become classics. They were based on the family cats, about whom Kathleen Hale – unable to find the sort of children's literature she wanted – devised stories for her sons.

The Orlando stories broke new ground in the way story-book cats were presented; however unlikely the plots, they contrive to seem entirely plausible in their self-consistent world. And they present family values in a rare way; whatever the multi-talented Orlando sets out to do – and he does many things – he is always supported by his dear wife, Grace, and never forgets the needs of his family.

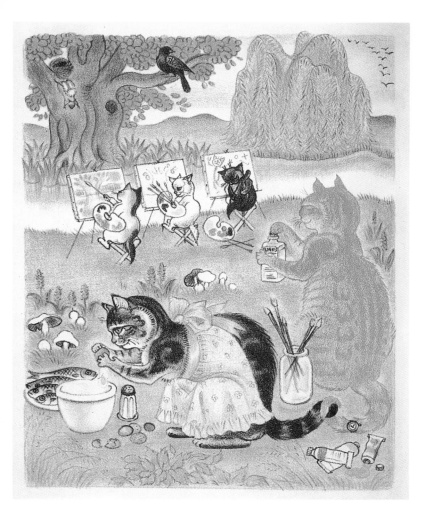

'The kittens spent the afternoon painting the view from the banks of the stream, and very good pictures they were. Pansy's was as nice upside down as right way up. Meanwhile, Grace prepared the supper.' This scene from the first Orlando book *A Camping Holiday* (1938) epitomises Orlando's idyllic world and the unity of his family.

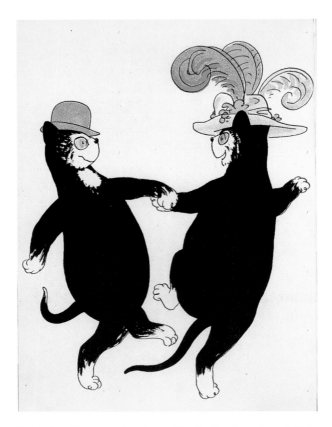

Eliot's first illustrator (1940) was Nicolas Bentley, whose Jellicle Cats adorn the dust wrapper and front cover for the very good reason that they are, without doubt, the most animated of his Practical Cat illustrations:

> 'Jellicle Cats come out to-night,
> Jellicle Cats come one come all:
> The Jellicle Moon is shining bright
> Jellicles come to the Jellicle Ball. . . .'

And there he is with his high-crowned bowler, and she with her Marie Lloyd plumes, showing everyone how to jive.

Old Possum's Book Of Practical Cats

In 1936, TS Eliot (1888–1965) announced *Mr Eliot's Book of Pollicle Dogs and Jellicle Cats as Recited to Him by the Man in White Spats*. It appeared three years later as *Old Possum's Book of Practical Cats*, evidence of the lesser-known playfulness of TS Eliot, the Modern Poet. It is not really a children's book, though some of the cats have a juvenile appeal. Skimbleshanks the Railway Cat (a parody of Kipling's *l'Envoi*), and Macavity the Mystery Cat are well known outside the Eliot circle.

'He can play any trick with a cork
Or a spoon and a bit of fish-paste . . .'
Edward Gorey's Mr Mistofelees,
The Original Conjuring Cat
Here performs levitational feats
How incredible – 'Just like that!'
(1957).

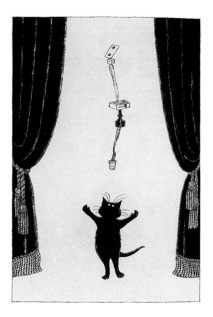

The Cat in the Hat

The revolutionary and surreal children's reader by Dr Seuss (Theodore Seuss Geisel, 1904–1991) appeared in 1957. It was revolutionary because it was designed to teach reading through humour, rhyme, repetition and pictures; the story was surreal.

Sally and her elder brother are home alone; it is too wet to go out to play. Suddenly, in walks the Cat in the Hat and sets up an elaborate balancing trick (as shown opposite) which fails. The Cat then produces a box containing two Things (Thing One and Thing Two) who fly kites indoors and cause further damage. The Cat packs the Things away in the box and leaves: this pleases the Goldfish, who has been driven to distraction by the Cat and his goings on, but there is still a terrible mess. The Cat returns riding on a vehicle with flexible arms which clear up the house just as Mother returns.

The Cat as depicted is not very appealing, but he's a storytelling device – a word on which to hang the lilting rhythm of the text – so perhaps we can forgive him.

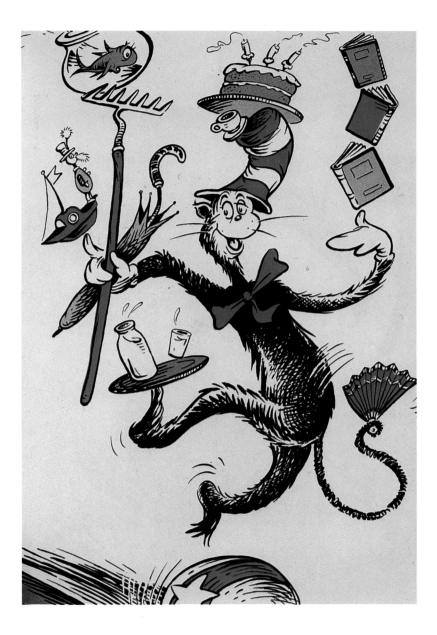

Searle's Big Fat Cats

Here are two fat cats by the British illustrator Ronald Searle. His intricately detailed style presents a world where his subjects are sometimes cats behaving in a human way; sometimes cats as seen by humans. In the former world, his cats ride horses, perform the can-can or play musical instruments; in his latter, they take over the world *(The Coming of the Great Cat God)* or can dream only of fish when confronted with an unsuitable banquet. The expressions on the cats' faces, and the predicaments in which they find themselves, are reminiscent of Louis Wain's cats at the beginning of the century [page 78] – which is a reflection of the way both artists studied their subjects and interpreted their observations in their own styles.

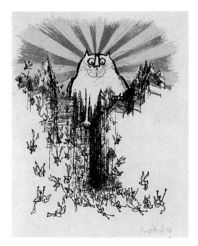

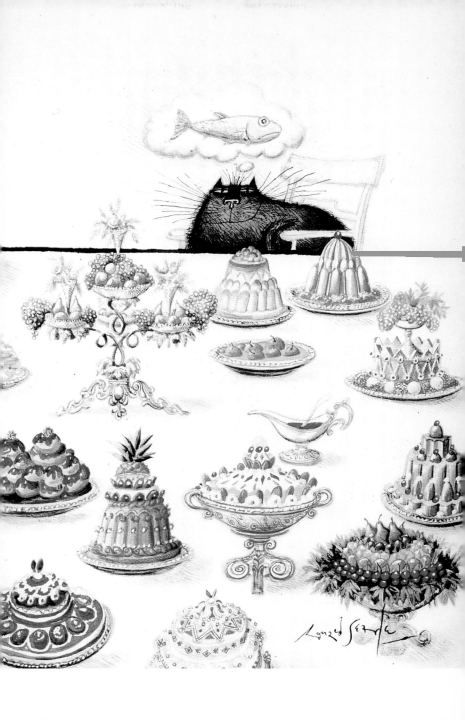

The Church Mice

Graham Oakley's series of delightful books about the Church Mice are equally about their protector and friend Sampson the Church Cat. Like Kathleen Hale [page 96], Graham Oakley writes of a world where the cat is entirely feline, yet behaves in a human way, and interacts believably with a human world. But whereas Orlando instigates the adventures in which he and his family take part, the adventures of Sampson and the Mice are outside their control and they have to devote their ingenuity to setting things right.

In *The Church Mice Adrift,* old Wortlethorpe is being redeveloped (it is 1976) and the rats displaced from the historic buildings take over the church where Sampson and the Mice live, driving them out to an empty house. Fortunately, there are still some things left there, including a dolls' house. This gives Sampson a bright idea, and he sets the Mice on to turning it into an floating Riverside Rataurant, with copious supplies of attractive garbage – all free. Along come the rats . . . gobble gobble . . . the dolls' house is cast adrift, and the rats are sent floating down the river. Unfortunately, two of the Mouse waiters fail to disembark in time, and are driven up on to the roof of the dolls' house by the angry rats. Sampson runs off to an overhanging willow tree to rescue them, with the aid of a party of Mice to help weigh the branch down. The two Mice succeed in scrambling on to Sampson's tail, but the willow bark strips and breaks. Luckily, they fall on to a passing punt and conclude their adventure by returning to their old home in Wortlethorpe church (although Sampson isn't best pleased at having his tummy tickled by the girl in the punt).

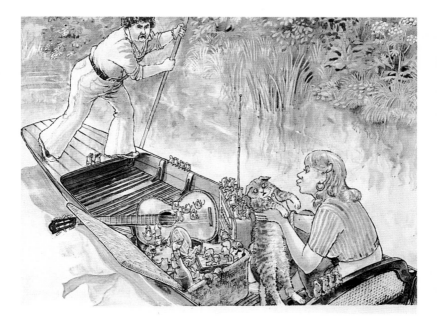

Kliban and Davis

We conclude our survey with illustrators Bernard Kliban and Jim Davis. They look at cats in different ways as shown by our two illustrations. Below is Kliban – perhaps the speaker in the armchair – explaining (in a parody of one who does drugs) how he became a cat person. Davis's world-weary (but world syndicated) Garfield, on the other hand, (opposite) is a solo cat very much in charge, dedicated to eating, sleeping, and commenting on the foibles of the humans with whom he comes into contact.

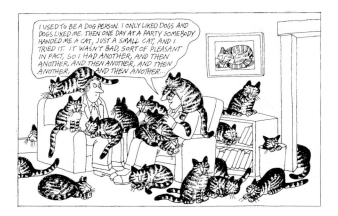

At the end of our 1,200-year journey, these two remind us that illustrative styles may have changed, and the lot of the cat has certainly changed, but perceptive illustrators have always understood the essence of being a cat.

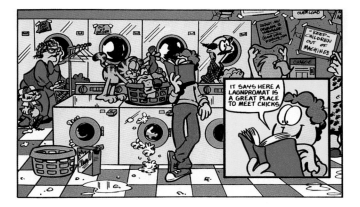

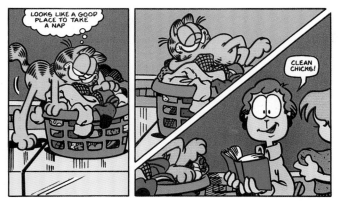

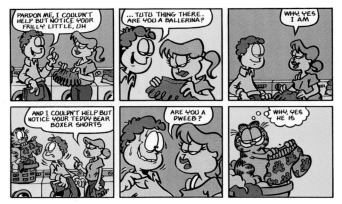

Picture Sources

[End papers] *Funny Pussies & True Stories* 1897 (BL 12809.w.24); [i] *Puss in Boots* ill R Heighway 1895 (BL 012808.ee.51/6); [Frontispiece] *Daddy Cat* Louis Wain 1915; [iii & 7–13] *Henriette Ronner* MH Spielmann 1895 (BL 7875.r.6); [iv] *The Cat and the Mouse* ill Alice B Woodward 1899 (BL 12809.o.20); [v] *The White Cat* 1847 see [59]; [6] 'Mischievous Kittens' Henriette Ronner 1891 (BL L404.m.1); [14] *The Lindisfarne Gospels* c700 (BL Cotton MS Nero DIV); [16] *The Book of Kells* c800 (The Board of Trinity College, Dublin); [18] *The Luttrell Psalter* c1330 (BL Add MS 42310); [19] Bestiary late C12 (BL Add MS 11283 f15),

Harleian Bestiary c1255 (BL Harley 3244 f49v); [20] Sketches by Leonardo da Vinci 1478 (© British Museum); [22] *Æsop's Fables* William Caxton 1484 (BL C.11.c.17); [24] *Adam & Eve* Albrecht Dürer 1504 (© British Museum); [26] *Aristotle* 1545 (BL 520.b.10); *The Historie of Foure-footed Beasts* Edward Topsell 1607 (BL 444.i.4); [27] *Emblemes* George Wither(s) 1635 (BL C.70.h.5); [28] *A Detection of Damnable Driftes, Practized by Three VVitches . . .* (The Chelmsford Witchcraft Trials) 1579 (BL C.27.a.8); [29] MS record of the Revd Miles Gale 1647 (BL Add MS 32496); [31, 33, 34 & 37] *Dick Whittington and His Cat* 1845 (BL 012806.ee.8); [32 & 35] *Dick Whittington and His Cat* ill John Proctor 1888 (BL 12800.f.45/5); [36] *Whittington and His Cat* 1874 (BL 12805.i.38); [38] *Æsop's Fables* Wenceslaus Hollar c1751 (BL 1872.a.12); [40] *The Cats' Concert* William Mulready 1808 (BL C.40.a.57); [42] *The Book of the Cat* Frances Simpson 1903; [43] *Collection des Mammifères du Muséum d'Histoire Naturelle* Jean Baptiste Huet 1808 (BL 461.l.3); [44] *Natural History of British Quadrupeds* Edward Donovan 1820

(BL 972.l.4); [46] *Fables* La Fontaine ill Grandville 1839 (BL 12304.g.14); [48] *Les Animaux Historiques* Otaire Fournier ill Victor Adam 1845 (BL 7205.d.7), 1884 (BL 7204.aa.8); [52] *Puss in Boots* ill R Heighway (BL 012808.ee.51/6); [53 & 55] 1858 (BL 12807.e.35); [54] 1991 by kind permission of the illustrator, Fred Marcellino; [56] ill Otto Spekter 1847 (BL 12809.f.57); [57] ill Otto Spekter 1856 (BL 1210.e.41); [58] *The White Cat* Marie La Mothe, Countess d'Aulnoy ill 'JW' 1847 (BL 551.f.14); [60] *Struwwelpeter* Heinrich Hoffmann-Donner 1847 (BL 12812.b.19); [62] *The Comical Creatures of Wurtemberg* ill Harrison Weir 1851 (BL 12806.e.47); [63] *The Pleasure Book of Domestic Animals* ill Harrison Weir 1865 (BL 12807.g.33), *Shireen & Her Friends* Gordon Stables ill Harrison Weir 1895 (BL 012807.ff.62); [64] *Adventures de Dame Trot* (French) 1858 (BL 12808.a.15); *The Comic Adventures of Dame Trot and her Cat* ill Will Gibbons 1888 (BL 12800.f.45/4); [67] *Alice's Adventures in Wonderland* Lewis Carroll ill John Tenniel 1865 (BL 12837.b.26); [68] ill Harry Rountree 1928; [69] ill Arthur Rackham 1907 (Reproduced by kind permission of his family); [70] Private collection; [71]

Nonsense Songs, Stories, Botany and Alphabets Edward Lear 1871 (BL C.116.e.22); [74] *Pussies at Mischief* 1873 (BL 12806.h.57); [75] *Pussie Cat's ABC Book* 1880 (BL 12805.n.30); [77] *The House that Jack Built* ill Randolph Caldecott 1876 (BL 12805.k.61); [79,80, 82 & 83] Private collection; [81] *ILN* Vol 85 p365 1884 (BL PP7611); [84] *Henriette Ronner* MH Spielmann 1895 (BL 7875.r.6); [86] *Bon Mots* Smith & Sheridan ill Aubrey Beardsley; [87] *Tales of Mystery and Imagination* 'The Black Cat' Edgar Allen Poe ill Aubrey Beardsley; [89] *Just-So Stories* 'The Cat that Walked by Himself' Rudyard Kipling 1902 (BL); [91] *The Roly-Poly Pudding* or *The Tale of Samuel Whiskers* Beatrix Potter (© copyright Frederick Warne & Co 1908, 1987); [92] *The White Kitten Book* ill Cecil Aldin 1909; [93] *Four Little Kittens* set up & photographed by Harry Whittier Freese 1934; [95] *Krazy Kat* George Herriman 1935 (By kind permission of King Features via Yaffa Licencing); [97] *Orlando the Marmalade Cat: A Seaside Holiday* Kathleen Hale* (© Kathleen Hale 1938, 1959, 1990. Reproduced by kind permission of Frederick Warne); [98] *Old Possum's Book of Practical Cats* TS Eliot

ill Nicolas Bentley 1940
(reproduced by permission
of Faber & Faber Ltd); [99] ill
Edward Gorey 1957 (©
Copyright Edward Gorey.
Reproduced by kind permis-
sion of Harcourt Brace &
Company); [100] *The Cat in
the Hat* Dr Seuss 1957; [102]
*Ronald Searle's Big Fat Cat
Book* 1967; [104] *The Church
Mice Adrift* Graham Oakley**
1976 (© Graham Oakley.
Reproduced by kind permis-
sion of Macmillan Children's
Books); [106] Cartoon by B
Kliban (© 1993 by Judith
Kamman Kliban. Used by
permission of Workman
Publishing Company, Inc);
[107] Cartoon by Jim Davis
(© Jim Davis, reproduced by
permission of Universal
Press Syndicate).

*Other Orlando titles
include: *Orlando the
Marmalade Cat: His Silver
Wedding, Orlando Buys a
Farm, Orlando Keeps a Dog,
Orlando and the Three Graces,
Orlando's Evening Out,
Orlando's Home Life.*

**Other Sampson titles
include: *The Church Mouse,
The Church Cat Abroad, The
Church Mice Spread Their
Wings, The Church Mice and
the Moon, The Church Mice at
Bay, The Church Mice at
Christmas, The Diary of a
Church Mouse, The Church
Mice and the Ring.*

Acknowledgements

Every project needs its sponsor, and I would like to thank David Way of British Library Publishing for his unflagging enthusiasm. It is delightful to have the resources of the British Library at one's disposal, but I could have made little use of them without Kathy Houghton who has obtained numerous catty books for inspection, arranged photography, and provided a variety of essential information. I am also most grateful to designer Roger Davies, who has presented our mixed bag of material in such a such a delightful and coherent way.

Thanks also to Miranda & Roger Pratt of Hereward Books for the cheerful freedom of their reference shelves, Michael & Valerie Grosvenor Myer for their ready discussion, and Kitty Platt for running the Cheshire Cat to earth.

As always, I owe an immense debt to my wife Judith, to whom I dedicate this book.

RODNEY DALE

Haddenham, Cambridgeshire

June 1997